# Encyclopedia One

## A Picture Book Encyclopedia

### Exploring the World in Stories and Pictures
### Volume 1

**Mossaab Shuraih MD**

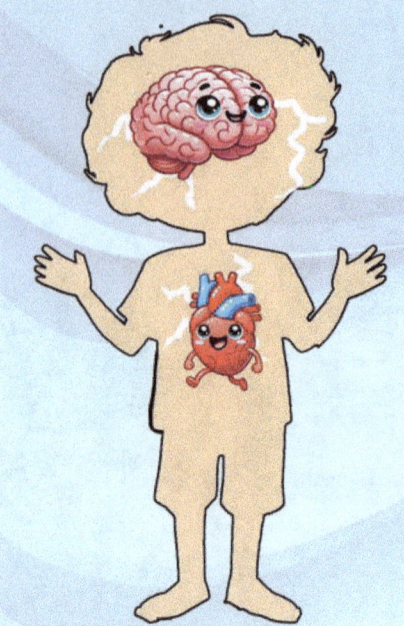

Copyright © 2025 Mossaab Shuraih

ISBN: 978-0-9899496-7-5

All rights reserved. No part of this book may be reproduced, distributed, or transmitted in any form or by any means, including photocopying, recording, or other electronic or mechanical methods, without the prior written permission of the publisher, except in the case of brief quotations embodied in critical reviews and certain other noncommercial uses permitted by copyright law.

This book is intended for informational and educational purposes only. While every effort has been made to ensure the accuracy and safety of the content, the author and publisher accept no responsibility for any injuries, damages, or losses that may occur as a result of following the information, experiments, or activities contained herein. Adult supervision is recommended for all activities and experiments. Readers are encouraged to exercise caution and seek professional advice if needed

Contact email: mshuraih@yahoo.com
Author :Mossaab Shuraih
Illustrator: Mossaab Shuraih with aid of AI technology

## Preface

As a father, I've always wanted to broaden my kids' horizons and nurture their critical thinking. When traditional children's encyclopedias with dense text failed to capture my son's interest, I realized the need for a colorful, engaging, storytelling encyclopedia that would feel like a picture book. That's how "Encyclopedia One" was born.

Using my background in graphic design and sketching, along with the incredible possibilities of AI-generated illustrations, I set out to craft a book that brings knowledge to life. Each page is designed to spark curiosity with concise, exciting topics that young minds can explore with joy and enthusiasm.

My son, now eight, loves the book, finding joy in exploring its pages, some of which answered his own questions. Together, we're now working on more books in this series. We hope Encyclopedia One captures your child's imagination as it has for my son, encouraging them to explore, question, and discover. Thank you for allowing this book to be a part of your family's journey of learning.

Dedicated to my two boys, who inspire my every word.
and to my wife, whose love and support make everything possible.

# Table of content

- The Big Bang ..................... 1
- Planet earth ..................... 5
- Australia ..................... 12
- Solar System ..................... 17
- Calendars ..................... 20
- The Story of Gravity ............. 29
- The Mona Lisa ..................... 33
- The Atom. ..................... 36
- Electricity ..................... 40
- The Roman Empire ............. 47
- Honey Bees ..................... 57
- Great Wall of China. ............. 62
- Albert Einstein ..................... 67
- Dinosaurs ..................... 72
- The Oxygen ..................... 80
- The Octopus ..................... 85
- Africa ..................... 86

# Table of content

- Archimedes …................... 92

- The Age of Discovery. …....... 99

- Social Skills. …................... 108

- Message to Aliens …........... 111

- The Story of Money …........... 116

- Alexander the Great …......... 121

- Life of Squirrels. …................ 125

- How Computers Think …....... 127

- Rainbows …..................... 130

- Heart Electricity …............... 134

- Human Brain …................. 136

- Healthy Habit. …................. 139

- Nobel Prize …................... 140

- Between Myth and Reality: Atlantis 144

A long long time ago …
Billions of years ago there was nothing
There were no stars
No earth
No moon
No people
No animals or trees
Not even a light it was just dark

# THE BIG BANG

And suddenly there was a huge explosion "BOOOM!!" that explosion is called the Big BANG! The fire and the energy from that big bang started to expand and expand till this very day!

The Big Bang was not just any explosion; it was the beginning of everything! From this fantastic event, all the stars, the sun, the moon, the Earth, and even the air we breathe started to form.

The Big Bang is the moment when the entire universe was born. Scientists believe this incredible event happened about 14 billion years ago. Since then, the universe has been stretching, growing, and expanding like a giant balloon, and it's still expanding as we speak!

Hello there! I'm Professor Gregory Bookbinder. I absolutely love exploring, reading, and sharing the fascinating things I learn with friends like you who have curious minds! If you love discovering the wonders of the world, come join me on this exciting adventure!

So, my dear friend, you, me, and everyone you've ever known or heard of live on this tiny blue sphere floating in the vastness of space, our incredible planet Earth!
Here's a mind-blowing fact: Earth is **4.5 billion years old**! But humanity? We've only been around for the last **200,000 years**. That's like a blink of an eye in Earth's history.
It's incredible to think about how new we are.

# Planet Earth

Now, see those vast stretches of blue? Those are our **Oceans** and seas. And the colorful patches of yellow and green? They're called **Continents.**

Continents are like gigantic puzzle pieces! That's where all our bustling cities, charming towns, sleepy villages, and lost history find their homes!

There are seven continents in the world:
1. North America
2. South America
3. Africa
4. Asia
5. Europe
6. Australia
7. Antarctica

**Seventy percent of Earth's surface is water,** mainly in the oceans. Beneath the ocean's surface, you can find mountains, volcanoes, and even rivers hiding in the deep!

Did you know that Earth makes humming sounds? Scientists have discovered that Earth makes a mysterious low-humming sound called the **Earth's Hum**. It's so low that we can't hear it with our ears!

The Earth spins very fast, at about 1,000 miles per hour at the equator! We don't feel it because we're spinning right along with it.

Planet Earth resembles a massive sphere with layers, similar to an onion. These layers form the Earth's interior: the Crust, Mantle, Outer Core, and Inner Core.

**Crust:** Outer layer. The crust is like the skin of an apple, thin compared to the other layers. All our families, friends, cities, animals, and even plants live on this thin part of the Earth. Incredibly, everything we see above ground happens on the crust!

**The Mantle:** the mantel is the largest layer of the Earth! It's made of very hot, soft rocks near the top and liquid-like rocks at the bottom, called **magma.** This layer is so big and powerful that it helps move the tectonic plates on the surface and causes volcanic eruptions!

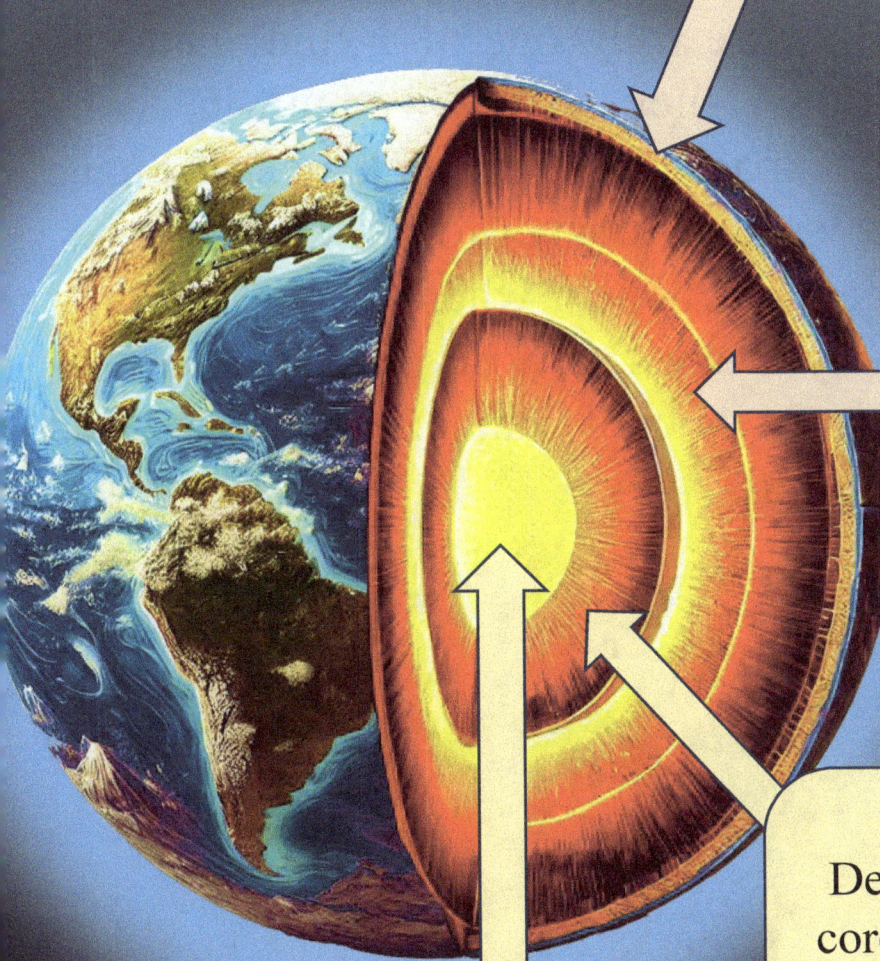

**The Outer Core**
Deeper down, we reach the outer core, made of liquid metal, mostly iron and nickel. It is super hot there . The outer core creates Earth's magnetic field.

**The Inner Core:** At the very center of Earth is the **inner core**, the hottest and hardest part! It's a solid ball made of **iron** and **nickel**; it is as hot as the surface of the Sun!

# Australia

Did you know that Australia is home to some of the most unique creatures on Earth? Yes, it is!

Kangaroos are some of the most fascinating animals in Australia, and they are truly one-of-a-kind! Did you know they have a built-in baby backpack? Yep, mama kangaroos have a special pocket on their tummies, called a pouch, where they carry their tiny babies. Those baby kangaroos have a cool name; they're called **'joeys!'**

Kangaroo super-duper power - the 'Big Hop'! They are super jumpers! They can hop really high, using their big long feet and strong tail.

Kangaroos are family-loving animals. They often go for pleasant night-time hops together under the moonlight.

The Kangaroo family has a special name. They are called the **Mob!**

"Koalas are another interesting animal in Australia."

The koala, an adorable and unique animal native to Australia, looks like a small teddy bear, but they are not actually bears. Koalas are marsupials, a group of animals that carry their babies in a pouch, just like kangaroos!

Koalas are super picky eaters; they eat only the leaves of one kind of tree, called Eucalyptus.

"Yoo" - rhymes with "you."
"Kuh" - like the "ca" in "cat."
"LIP" - rhymes with "sip."
"Tuhs" - rhymes with "bus."

Koalas like to spend their time in eucalyptus trees, where they sleep most of the day. They are big sleepyheads! They can sleep from 18 to 22 hours a day! I wish I could do the same sometimes.

You might think all the animals in Australia are cuddly types like koalas, but no! There is one animal that's a bit more on the wild side – the Tasmanian devil! This feisty fella isn't the hugging type at all; he's full of energy and has some serious attitude.

This little guy lives on a tiny island just next to Australia.

The Tasmanian devil has a loud growl and can produce high, eerie screams that used to startle people at night! That's how it earned the name "devil"—due to its frightening nighttime sounds.

But don't worry, they're not as scary as they sound. They're actually quite amazing. Tasmanian devils have super-strong teeth that can chew through almost anything. They can munch on bones and fur with ease. They're like the cleanup crew of the wild, ensuring nothing goes to waste. They're the eco-heroes with their powerful jaws!

They may not be the cuddle buddies you'd encounter in a storybook, but these Tasmanian devils are superstars in their own wild way! They clean their environment.

# The Solar System

Planet Earth is one of the eight amazing planets that spin around the Sun. Together with the Sun, these planets, their moons, and other cool space objects form what we call the **Solar System.**

At the heart of our solar system is the Sun, a medium-sized star with a big job! The Sun is a blazing ball of fire, constantly roaring with explosions and energy. These powerful blasts of light and heat brighten our skies. The Sun's gravity works like a magnet to keep all the planets perfectly in orbit, spinning around and around. Each planet in our solar system has its own quirky personality. Oh yes, they're like a cosmic cast of characters!

Mercury is the closest planet to the Sun and it's the smallest planet, but don't underestimate it! By day, it sizzles like a frying pan, and by night, it's freezing cold. Venus, the second planet, is the hottest planet in the solar system, wrapped in thick clouds and a heavy atmosphere that exerts crushing pressure and pours sulfuric acid rain, which is completely unfriendly to humans. Our beloved Earth is the third planet and the oasis of life in our solar system.

Mars, the Red Planet! Did you know **SpaceX and NASA** are gearing up to send brave astronauts to colonize Mars? Yep, it might just become humanity's second home someday! Scientists already sent a fleet of Robots to land on its surface, poking and rolling around to uncover its mysteries. These robotic buddies have been trying to study Mars and search for signs of possible life. It is believed that Mars once had water on its surface! Rivers, lakes, maybe even oceans!

Jupiter is the largest planet in the solar system, so big that it could fit all the other planets inside it. Its Great Red Spot is a giant storm that has been raging for hundreds of years. Saturn is famous for its beautiful rings; Saturn's rings are made of ice and rocks, and they're so wide that you could fit six Earths side by side across them!

The next planet is Uranus. It's frosty and the coldest planet in the solar system. It tried to copy Saturn with faint rings, but it has its own unique personality as it spins almost completely on its side, earning it the nickname 'The Sideways Planet'.

**Jupiter**        **Saturn**        **Vranus**        **Neptune**

Neptune, the eighth and farthest planet from the Sun, is icy, extremely cold, and home to some of the fastest winds in the solar system. For many years, the small rocky planet Pluto was considered the ninth planet in the solar system, but due to its very small size, Pluto was demoted to a dwarf planet, breaking the hearts of Pluto fans everywhere!

> Let me tell you about one of my favorite subjects of all time: THE CALNEDAR!

# Calendars

A day is the time it takes for Earth to spin once around its axis.

A year is the time it takes for Earth to orbit around the Sun.

Calendars are tools that people use to track time, days, months, and years. A year is the duration it takes for Earth to complete one full revolution around the sun. Each time Earth finishes this cycle, a year has passed.

This book was published in the year **2025**. Does that mean Earth has gone around the sun **2,025 times only**? Not exactly! Scientists believe Earth is about **4.5 billion years old**, so why do we call this year 2025? Where are the rest of the billions of years !

Let's explore the captivating history of how calendars were developed and how we arrived at the system we use today.

Ancient people observed nature and noticed patterns that repeated themselves. They used these patterns to count days, months, and years. One of the earliest tools they used was the moon. Since the moon changes shape every day and completes its cycle every 28–30 days, they created what's called a **Lunar Calendar** to track time.

The ancient Egyptians lived along the Nile River, and their lives revolved around its cycles. They observed that the Nile would flood at the same time each year, and this flooding was important because it made the soil fertile for growing crops.

To plan their farming, the Egyptians created a calendar based on the seasons and the Sun, which we now call the **Solar Calendar.**

The Egyptian **solar calendar** consisted of 365 days and was divided into three seasons, each lasting four months:
**Flood Season:** The period when the Nile flooded.
**Planting Season:** The time for sowing seeds in the rich soil.
**Harvest Season:** The time for gathering crops.

Each month had 30 days, resulting in a total of 360 days. But wait! There are 365 days in a year, right? The Egyptians added 5 extra days at the end of the year, which they used for festivals to honor their gods!

**How Did They Know When the Year Began?** The Egyptians were amazing astronomers. They observed that the star Sirius (the brightest star in the night sky) would rise in the sky just before sunrise every year, right before the Nile began to flood. They used this as the beginning of their year!

**Why Is the Egyptian Solar Calendar Important?**

The Egyptian calendar was one of the first to use the **365-day year**, which influenced the calendars we use today, like the **Gregorian calendar**. Their understanding of time was so advanced that it helped them build their amazing monuments, such as the pyramids and temples, with incredible precision.

**Julius Caesar,** one of the most famous Roman generals, visited Egypt and admired the Egyptian calendar. At that time, the Roman calendar had only 10 months. Impressed by the accuracy of the Egyptian solar calendar, he decided to reform the Roman calendar using a similar approach!

Julius Caesar adopted the 365-day year, similar to the Egyptians. He introduced a leap year every four years to compensate for the extra 0.25 days in the solar year, which the Egyptians did not account for. He divided the year into 12 months with lengths similar to today's calendar. Julius Caesar even named a month after himself: "July."

This new system became the Julian calendar, which served as the basis for the calendar we use today, Hundreds of years later, in **1582**, Pope **Gregory XIII** made another tweak to keep the calendar even more accurate. This became the **Gregorian Calendar**, which most of the world uses today.

Thousands of years ago, a civilization called the Maya flourished in Central America. They created their calendar, which was fascinating because it used the moon, the sun, and the stars to predict the seasons and plan their rituals. Not only that, but they also had a Long Count Calendar that could predict natural events hundreds and even thousands of years into the future, like solar eclipses, with remarkable accuracy!

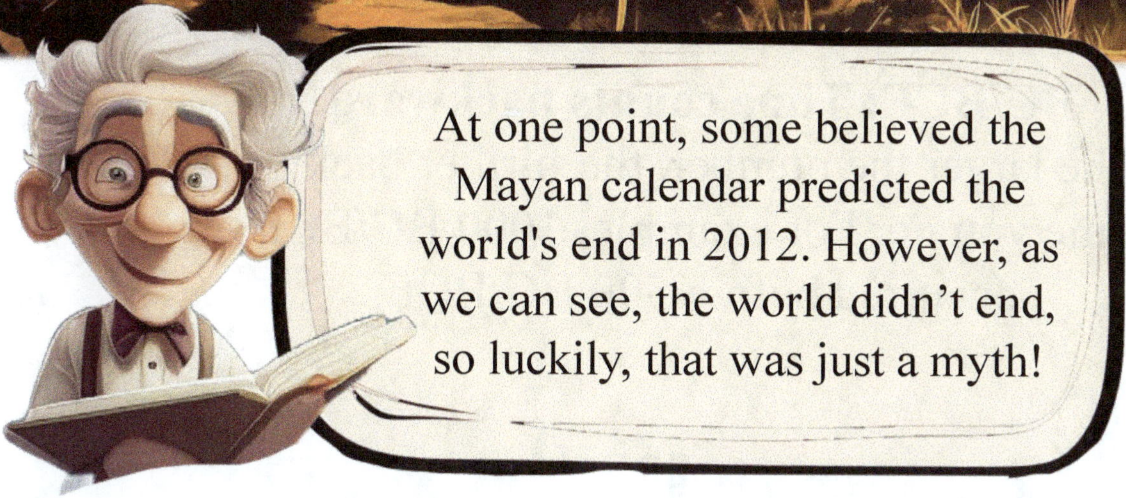

At one point, some believed the Mayan calendar predicted the world's end in 2012. However, as we can see, the world didn't end, so luckily, that was just a myth!

# What does the terms BC, AD or BCE CE mean ?

**BC:** It stands for **"Before Christ."** It counts the years before Jesus Christ was born. Example: The pyramids in Egypt were built around 2500 BC, a long, long time ago!

There are newer terms that mean the same thing as BC and AD, but they don't refer specifically to Jesus. They're used to make history more inclusive for everyone.

**BCE** stands for **"Before Common Era."** It is equivalent to **BC**, counting the years prior to Year 1. For example, the construction of the Great Wall of China began in the 7th century BCE.

## BC / BCE time

2000　　　1500　　　1000　　　500

**BC/BCE: Time counts backward.**
The larger the number, the further back in time you go. For example, 1000 BC/BCE occurred before 500 BC/BCE.

**AD** stands for **"Anno Domini,"** which is Latin for **"In the Year of Our Lord."** It counts the years following the birth of Jesus Christ. For example, this book is published in the year 2025 AD.

There are also newer terms that convey the same meaning as AD, but they do not specifically reference Jesus. These terms aim to make history more inclusive for all.

**CE**: It stands for **"Common Era"**. It's the same as AD, counting the years after Year , for example: We're living in the year **2025 CE**.

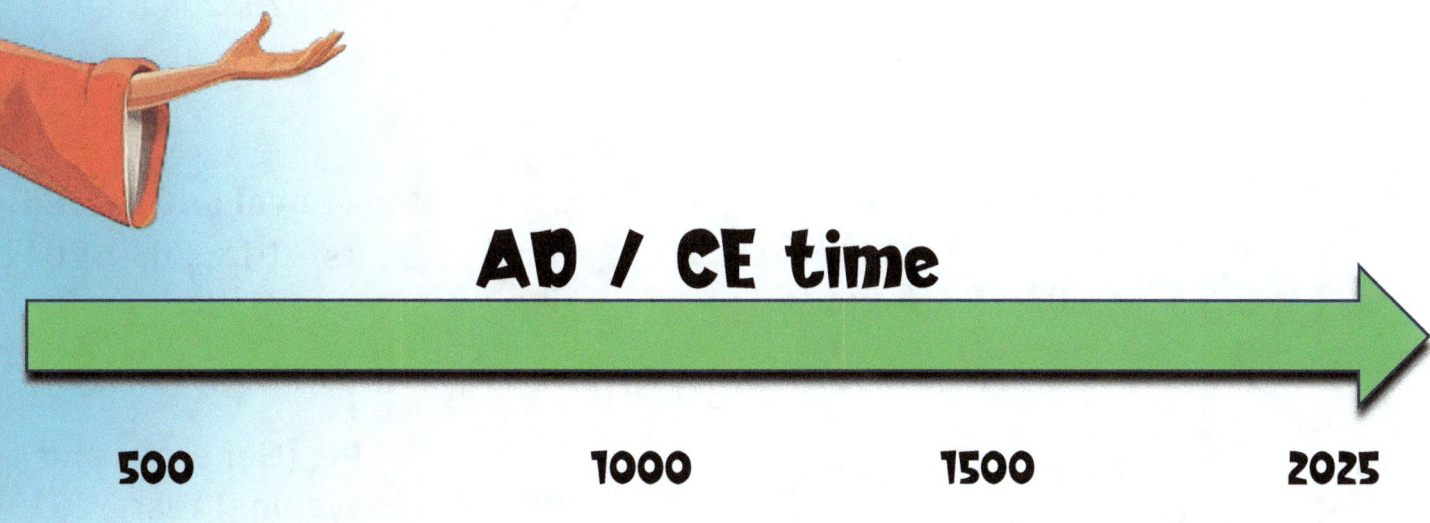

**AD/CE: Time counts forward.**
Just like the numbers on a calendar, the smaller the number, the further back in time you go. For example, 500 AD/CE occurred before 1000 AD/CE.

The Chinese calendar is another fascinating system that combines the moon and the sun (a lunar-solar calendar). One of the coolest things about the Chinese calendar is the **Chinese Zodiac**, where each year is connected to one of 12 animals. Each animal is believed to bring special qualities to people born in its year, making it a fun and meaningful tradition! Let's find out which year is yours!

**Tiger (Brave and Adventurous)** Years: 2010, 2022, 2034, etc.

**Monkey (Playful and Smart)** Years: 2016, 2028, 2040, etc

**Rabbit (Gentle and Kind)** Years: 2011, 2023, 2035, etc.

**Rooster (Confident and Hardworking)** Years: 2017, 2029, 2041, etc.

**Dragon (Powerful and Charismatic)** Years: 2012, 2024, 2036, etc.

**Dog (Loyal and Friendly)** Years: 2018, 2030, 2042, etc.

**Snake (Wise and Mysterious)** Years: 2013, 2025, 2037, etc.

**Pig (Generous and Easygoing)** Years: 2019, 2031, 2043, etc.

**Horse (Free-Spirited and Energetic)** Years: 2014, 2026, 2038, etc.

**Rat (Smart and Quick-Witted)** Years: 2008, 2020, 2032, etc.

**Goat (Kind and Creative)** Years: 2015, 2027, 2039, etc.

**Ox (Strong and Reliable)** Years: 2009, 2021, 2033, etc.

# The Story of Gravity

Long ago, in 17th-century England, there lived a curious man named Sir Isaac Newton. Newton loved to explore the world and was always full of questions about how things worked.

One day, while sitting under a tree, he noticed an apple fall to the ground. This simple moment made him wonder: Why did the apple fall straight down instead of sideways or upward? That one question sparked an idea that would change the course of human history forever: the discovery of gravity!

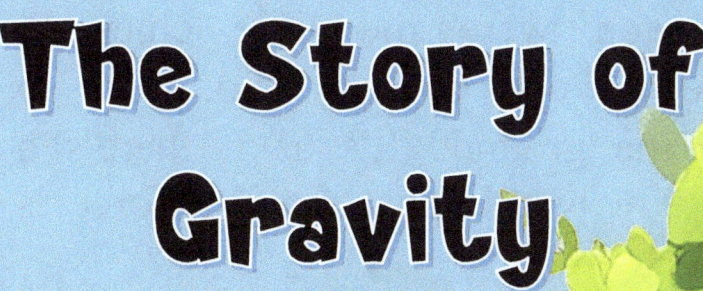

Ah, the falling apples of Newton were the little clues to understanding the invisible force we call **Gravity!** So, why do apples, or anything else, fall to the ground? It's as if there's a magical force pulling everything downward. That magical force is gravity!

Earth's gravity is the reason why all animals, people, and objects are attached to Earth, not floating in the sky; when space astronauts fly away from Earth, they are floating in space because they are far enough from the Earth that gravity does not affect them as much.

Do you want to learn something interesting? Isaac Newton, the person who discovered gravity, is also the one who helped humanity understand how to defy gravity and travel into space! Newton established laws that explain how objects move. One of those laws, known as Newton's Third Law of Motion, states that:

**For every Action, there is an equal and opposite Reaction.**

**Action**

**Reaction**

Let me explain: when you kick a ball against a wall, it strikes the wall with force in that direction. Then, the wall exerts an equal and opposite force, pushing the ball back. That's why the ball bounces off the wall! The harder you kick, the more the ball will rebound because the wall's opposing force is greater.

By understanding this law of motion and the Action-Reaction concept, humans have been able to build space rockets that overcome the force of gravity, allowing astronauts to travel into space.

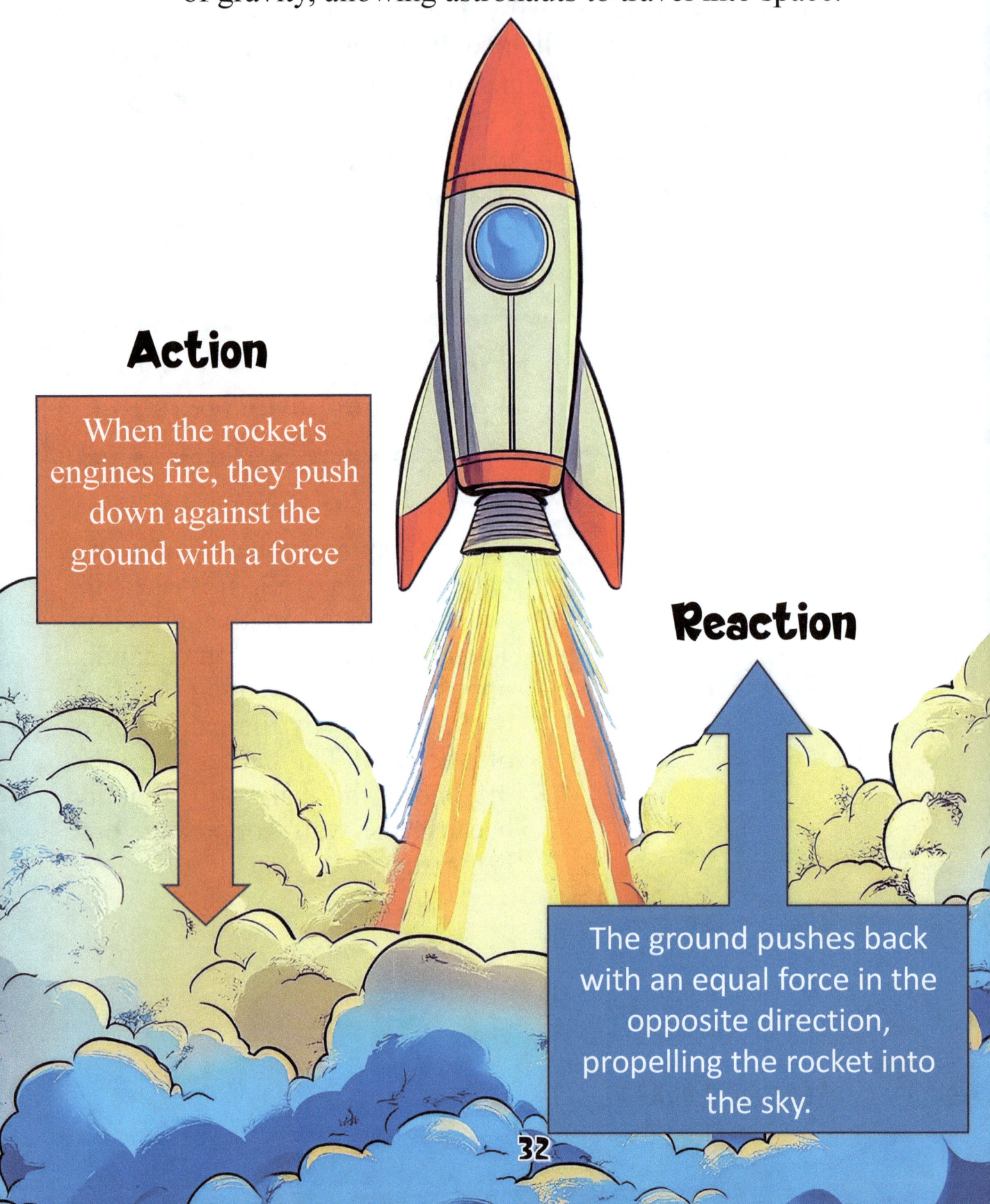

**Action**

When the rocket's engines fire, they push down against the ground with a force

**Reaction**

The ground pushes back with an equal force in the opposite direction, propelling the rocket into the sky.

# The Mona Lisa

Over 500 years ago, a wealthy man living in Italy wanted to have a painting of his wife, Lisa. He approached a famous artist at the time named **Leonardo da Vinci** and asked him to paint a portrait of his beautiful wife. Little did these two men know, that at that moment, they were creating what would become the most famous painting in the world.

Leonardo was not an ordinary artist; he was a genius, an artist, a scientist, and a visionary with ideas for many future inventions! That is a story by itself for a different day.

Leonardo started painting the **Mona Lisa.** He painted and painted, but he always found more details to add and things to modify, and it took him years and years to finish. Some say it took him over 14 years to complete.

Leonardo da Vinci didn't stay in Italy; eventually, he moved to Paris, France, where he lived under the protection of King Francis I, who admired Leonardo's art and knowledge and loved having him around.

When Leonardo passed away, the king took his paintings and kept them in Paris. The Mona Lisa remained in a museum for hundreds of years. During those years, it was not considered famous until one day, it mysteriously disappeared from the museum!

An Italian man who worked in Paris, France, managed to steal the painting from the museum. He hid it for two full years before the police found him and recovered the painting.

When the Mona Lisa returned to the museum, it became incredibly famous. People were astonished by the fact that it had been stolen and how it was eventually retrieved. Since that day, the Mona Lisa has become the most famous painting in the world, with millions of people visiting Paris to see it in the museum and take pictures of it.

# The Atom

Hey! Did you know that everything in the world is made up of zillions of tiny things called ATOMS? That's right! ATOMS

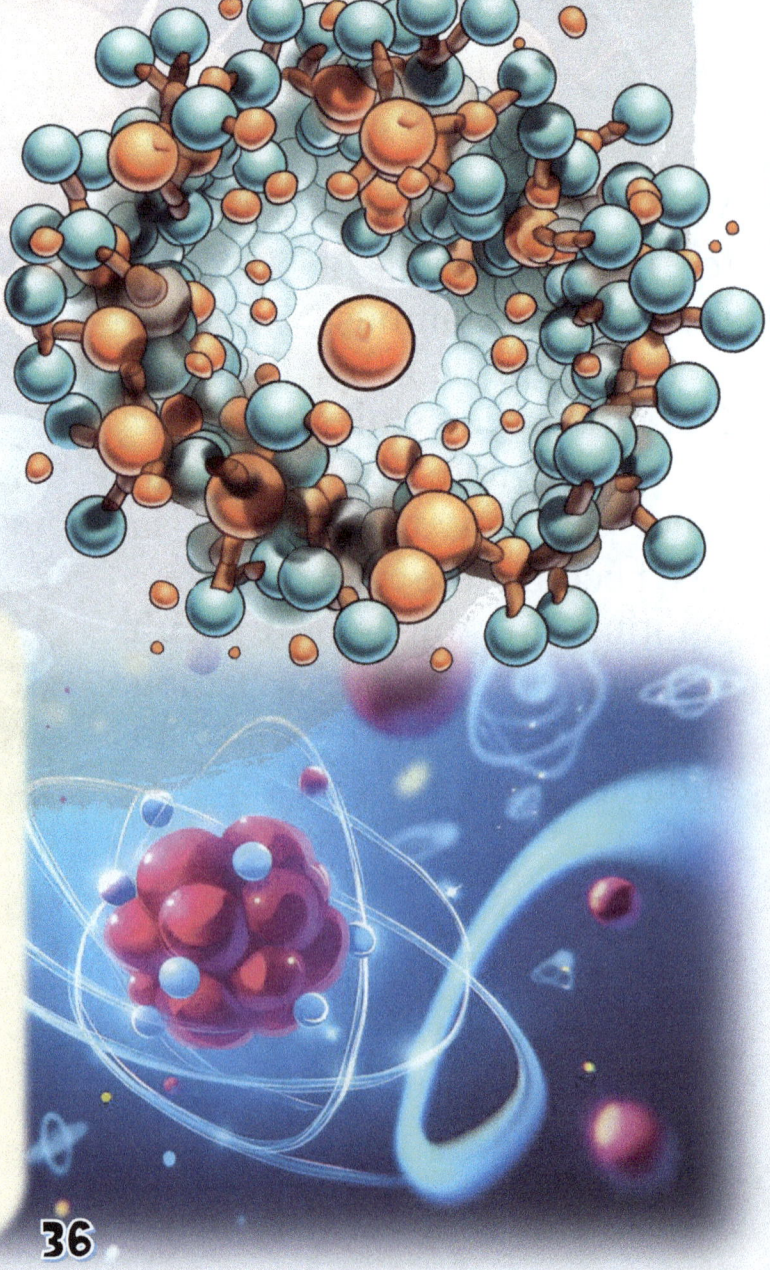

Atoms are like the magical building blocks of everything you see around you. Picture them as super-duper small specks, almost like tiny marbles, that clump together to make up every single thing in this world.

Atoms are super-duper tiny. But guess what?! They're not the smallest things in the universe. Nope, not even close! Inside each atom is a whole world of even tinier parts

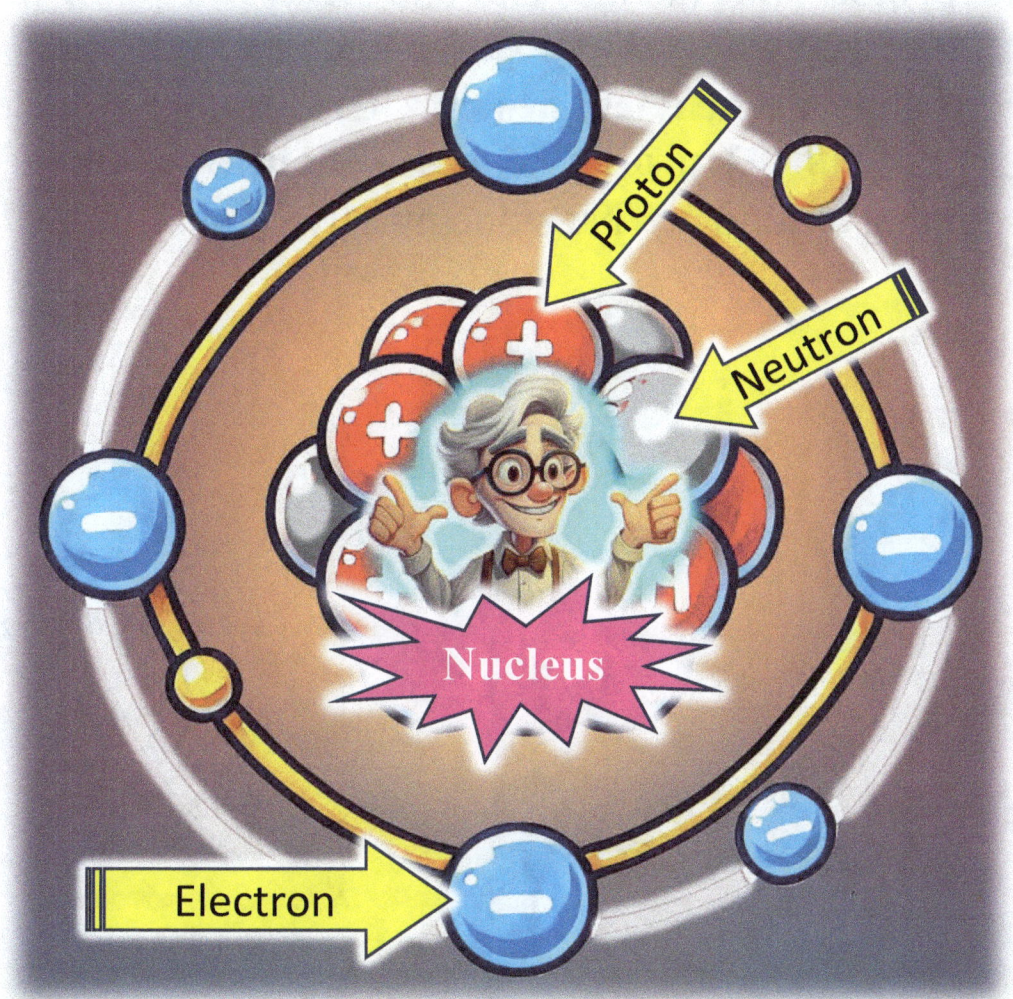

At the center of the atom sits the **Nucleus**, its cozy little sun. The nucleus is made up of two even smaller particles, **Protons** and **Neutrons**, snuggled together in the atom's center; now, imagine little planets zipping around this center at lightning speed; those are the **Electrons**!

- **Protons** are full of positive electrical energy (+)
- **Neutrons** are cool and chill; they don't carry any electrical charges
- **Electrons**, those speedy little particles, carry a negative electrical energy (-)

Atoms come in all sorts of sizes, depending on the number of **protons**, **neutrons**, and **electrons** they have. The **smallest atom** is **Hydrogen**, with just one **proton** in its nucleus and one **electron** zipping around it. It's tiny but mighty it's also the most common atom in the universe! On the other hand, the **heaviest atom** is **Uranium**. Its nucleus is a massive, packed with **92 protons** and **146 neutrons**, and it has **92 electrons** spinning around it. That's one massive atom!

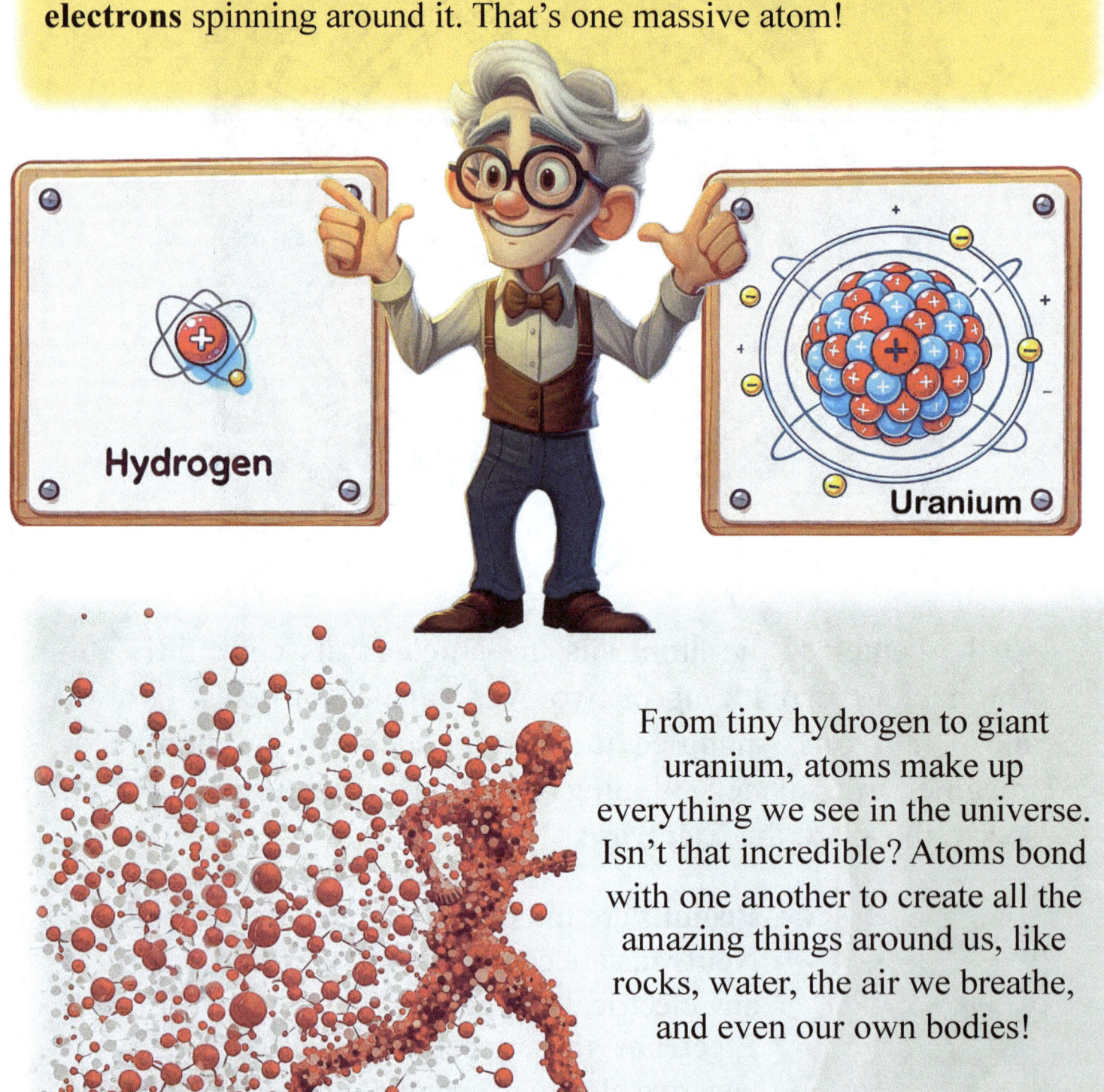

From tiny hydrogen to giant uranium, atoms make up everything we see in the universe. Isn't that incredible? Atoms bond with one another to create all the amazing things around us, like rocks, water, the air we breathe, and even our own bodies!

For example
Two hydrogen atoms bond with one oxygen atom to form water. That's why water is nicknamed **H2O**; it's made of 2 hydrogens (H2) and one oxygen (O).

Two oxygen atoms connect to form the oxygen **(O2)** we breathe in the air. Without it, we wouldn't survive!

When atoms come together, they create all the amazing materials around us, like food, shoes, water, and even the air we breathe!

It's incredible how these tiny building blocks team up to form everything we see and use every day.

# Electricity

Electricity is the magical power that makes everything work! It's why light bulbs turn on and shine, why phones and TVs work, and so many tools and devices come to life. Electricity is an important power that helps us every day!

Electricity is a type of energy that flows through tiny particles called **Electrons**. These electrons move around, and when they flow through wires or other materials, they create electricity. These electrons come from the atoms we talked about before!

Electricity is, in fact, a natural thing! It's found everywhere in nature: lightning during storms, in animals, and even within your own body. Lightning in the sky during a rainstorm is merely a massive electrical charge created by nature. Isn't that amazing?

Some animals have their own electric powers! **Electric eels** can generate electricity to shock predators and defend themselves.

Electricity also exists Inside Your Body! Did you know that your body uses electricity? Your Brain sends tiny electrical signals to your muscles to make them move. Your Heart beats because of electrical signals, too!

So, when did humans first learn about electricity, and how did they figure out how to use it?

People have known about electricity for a very long time! Around 600 BCE (the same as 600 BC), ancient Greeks noticed that when they rubbed a piece of **amber** (a type of tree resin) with fur, it could attract small objects like feathers. In fact, the word **'electricity'** comes from the Greek word **'elektron,'** which means amber!

Later, in 1752 AD (or CE), an American inventor and scientist performed a very dangerous experiment ( **DO NOT TRY THIS AT HOME**). He wanted to show that lightning is a form of electricity. To do this, he flew a kite with a metal key attached to it during a thunderstorm. When the key sparked, he proved that lightning and electricity are the same thing!

The first electrical battery was invented by an Italian scientist in 1800 His name was **Alessandro Volta**. He stacked layers of zinc and copper with pieces of salty water-soaked cardboard in between. This created a steady flow of electric current, which was a huge breakthrough! People realized they could make a continuous flow of electricity in the lab. To honor this brilliant Italian inventor, the unit of electric current strength is called the **Volt** (like in batteries has: 2 volts, 5 volts, and so on)

In 1831 AD, an English scientist named **Michael Faraday** discovered how to generate electricity using a magnet and a coil of wire! He built the first electric generator, demonstrating how moving a magnet near a wire could create an electric current.

This groundbreaking idea became the foundation of modern electricity generation, which we now achieve using power plants with turbines and magnets.

The famous American inventor Thomas Edison created the light bulb, among hundreds of other remarkable inventions. The electric light bulb was revolutionary because it allowed homes and factories to be lit at night. However, Edison encountered a challenge in delivering electricity to homes. While Thomas Edison was a brilliant inventor, he made one incorrect assumption about how electricity should be transmitted.

He believed transmitting electricity using a continuous flow of electrical charge, known as (Direct Current or DC), was the best way to deliver electricity to homes. However, it wasn't the ideal way to move electricity over long distances because it required more power and made the process harder.

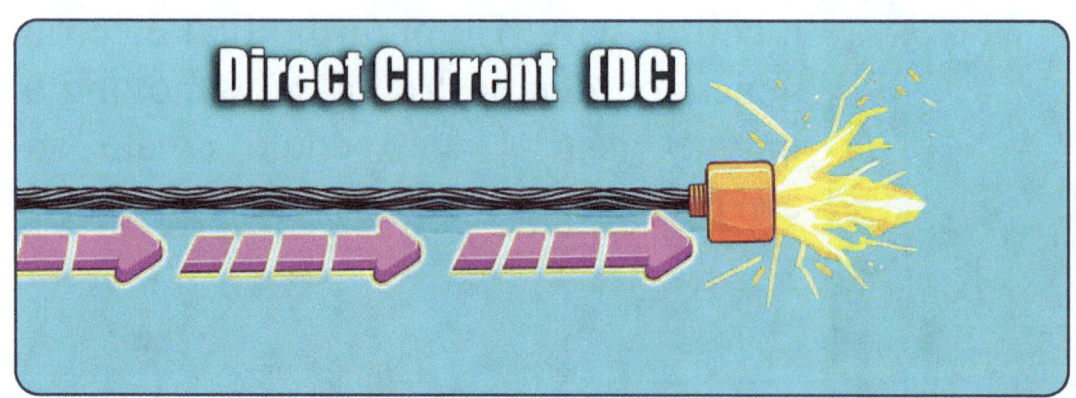

DC Current electricity flows in one direction like a river

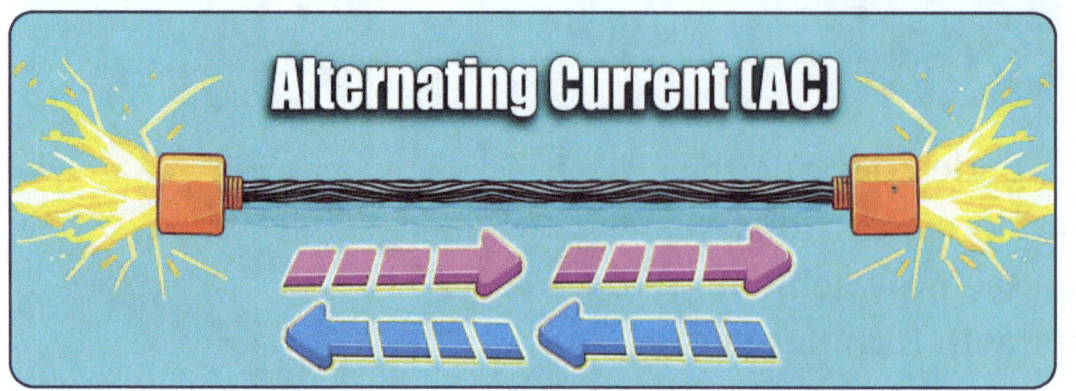

AC Current electricity flows back and forth directions like waves

Edison's assistant, another brilliant man with a fascinating and mysterious story, **Nikola Tesla,** had a different idea. Tesla believed that moving electricity back and forth (alternating current or AC) was a superior method. Although Tesla was a humble man, he possessed remarkable intelligence, had big dreams, and created numerous incredible inventions. He was also convinced that Edison was mistaken about direct current (DC).

Edison didn't like Tesla telling him what to do, and the two had huge arguments. But eventually, Tesla was proven right, showing that Alternating Current (AC) was the best way to move electricity!

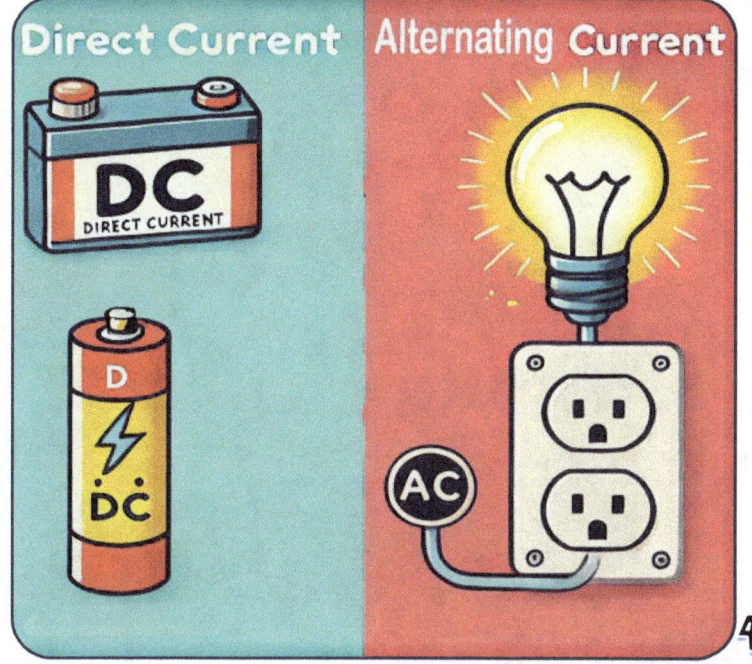

Today, we still use Tesla's method of transmitting electricity through Alternating Current (AC) to power our homes and cities. Meanwhile, smaller devices like batteries operate using Direct Current (DC). Both ways of transmitting electricity are important and make our lives better!

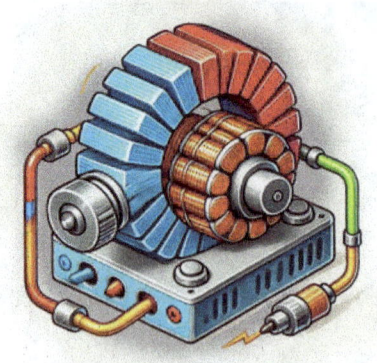

Most of our electricity these days comes from Faraday's discovery of spinning wires around magnets (or magnets around wires), and voilà! We get electricity!

But how do we get those generators to spin? Engineers have been coming up with all sorts of creative ideas! Some use heat and steam from burning fuels like coal, gas, or even wood to make engines spin wildly.

Others harness the power of nature, like using giant wind turbines to grab the wind's energy or building dams on rivers to let running water do the heavy lifting. It's like Mother Nature lending a helping hand to keep our lights on. Pretty neat, huh?"

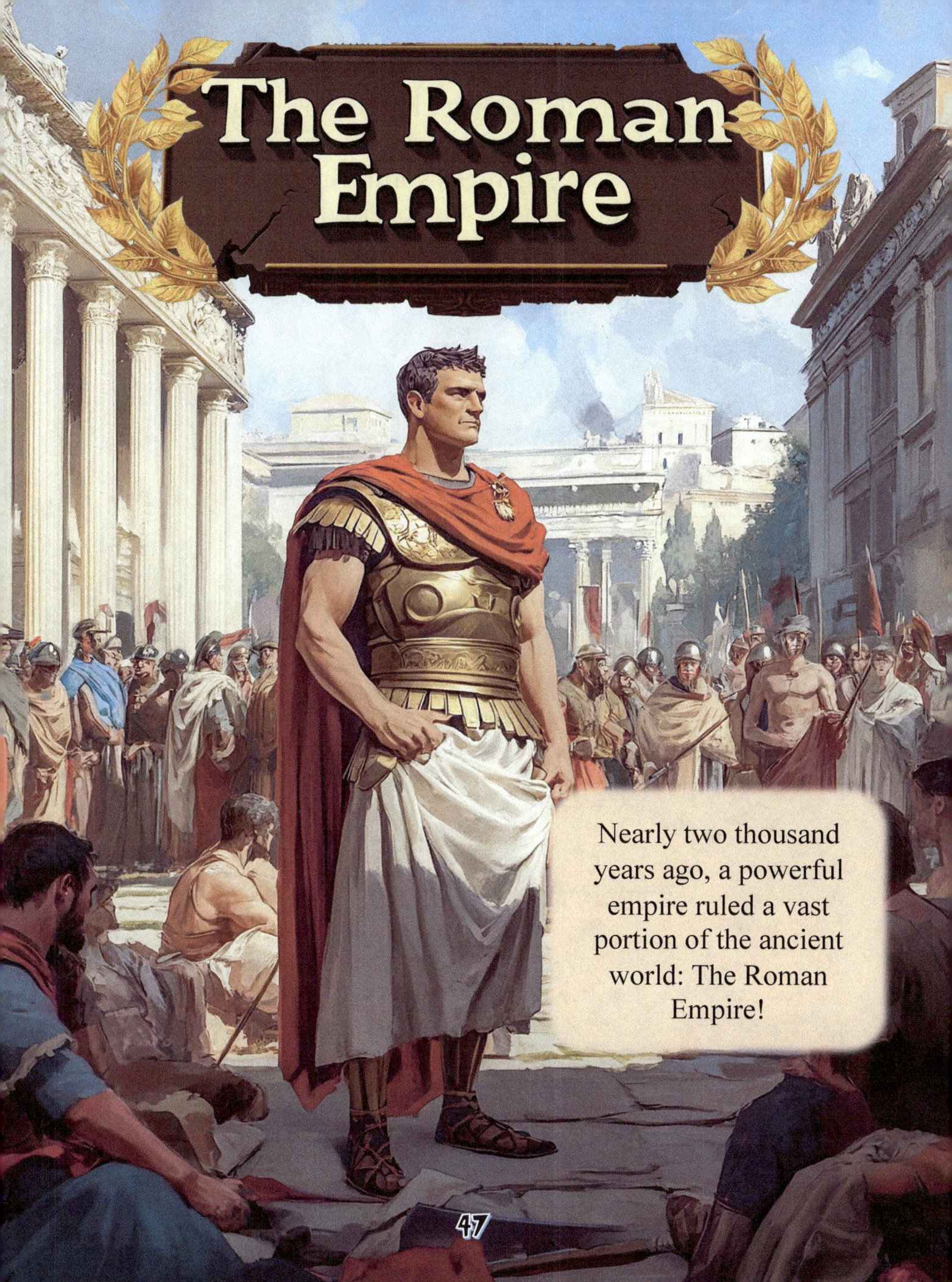

# The Roman Empire

Nearly two thousand years ago, a powerful empire ruled a vast portion of the ancient world: The Roman Empire!

With a mighty army, the Roman Empire grew to be one of the largest and most powerful empires the world had ever seen. The Empire stretched across Europe, North Africa, and the Middle East, spanning parts of 40 modern-day countries.

Let's dive into the fascinating history of the Roman Empire! How did it begin? What led to its fall? And why is it still so famous and important today? Prepare to discover the remarkable story of one of history's greatest civilizations!

Once upon a time, a she-wolf found two abandoned twin brothers, Romulus and Remus, by the banks of a flowing river. She nursed and raised them with care.

These two brothers would grow up to build the great city of Rome, marking the beginning of one of history's most legendary civilizations. This story may be a myth, but the city of Rome is undoubtedly real. Rome grew to become one of the greatest cities in history, filled with amazing stories.

the people of Rome said, 'We don't want kings bossing us around anymore!' So, they came up with a new government led by a group of rich and wise people called Senators. This system was known as the Roman Republic. With the Senate in charge, the Republic grew strong.

The Republican system worked well for 500 years. The republic had a large, strong army that invaded lands and countries to expand the empire. Rome was growing fast, conquering lands from Spain to Greece.

The city of Rome, first the heart of the Roman Republic and later the capital of the Roman Empire, was celebrated for its incredible beauty and grandeur. It was filled with majestic temples, grand theaters, and luxurious bathhouses, all crafted with stunning marble and stone. Rome truly stood as a symbol of power and sophistication.

To this day, Rome is still one of the most beautiful cities in the world to visit. As the capital of Italy, it's a place where you can walk among the ruins of the Roman Empire and feel the echoes of ancient history all around you.

With great power came great greed, and soon, problems started to pop up! While the army worked hard to expand the Republic, the wealthy senators enjoyed parties and a life of luxury in the grand city of Rome. The rich senators became even richer, while poor farmers struggled to get by.

Big-shot army generals like **Julius Caesar** became far more popular than the Senators, who were busy enjoying their cushy lives back in Rome. Julius Caesar was a brilliant general who famously conquered Gaul (modern-day France). But instead of retiring to a quiet life in the countryside to celebrate his victories, he had a bold idea: 'Why not rule Rome?'"

Julius Caesar marched into Rome with his army and took control of the city after a civil war. He was then named **Dictator for Life.** This marked the beginning of the end for the Roman Republic.

The Roman Republic was built on the idea that no one person should have too much power. The Senate was supposed to lead, with power shared among many senators. the senators didn't like the amount of power Julius Caesar had gained, so they conspired to get rid of him.

Following Julius Caesar's death, his adopted son, Octavian—later known as Augustus—waged a series of wars. In 27 BC, Octavian became the first Roman emperor, marking the official end of the Republic and the beginning of the Roman Empire.

The Roman Empire expanded and grew stronger, but with such growth came challenges. Managing such a vast empire wasn't easy. Some emperors were strong and wise, like Marcus Aurelius, who is remembered as one of Rome's greatest leaders for his fairness and wisdom.

However, not all emperors were as capable. Some were weak, and a few were downright crazy, like Nero, who is infamous for supposedly playing music while a massive fire ravaged much of the city of Rome. Stories even suggest that Nero may have started the fire himself, although history isn't entirely certain.

The Roman Empire became too large to manage, so it split into two: the **Western Roman Empire**, which ruled from Rome, and the Eastern Roman Empire, which ruled from **Constantinople**. The Western Empire fell in 476 AD after barbarian invasions, but the Eastern Empire, known as the **Byzantine Empire**, lasted another 1,000 years. It finally fell in 1453 AD when the Ottoman Turks conquered Constantinople

Let's talk about Honey Bees!

Honey bees are amazing little creatures! I know they can be a bit scary with their sting, but they are truly remarkable.

Honey bees like to live in big families called colonies, where they build beautiful hexagonal homes, known as hives. Within these hives, honey bees raise their babies and store the honey they produce. Thousands of bees work together to build and care for the hive, ensuring it remains healthy and running smoothly. Each bee has a specific role that helps keep everything running smoothly.

**The Queen Bee** – She is the boss of the hive. There's only one queen, and her job is to **lay eggs**, which turn into new bees. She can lay up to 2,000 eggs a day. That's like laying a baby bee every 40 seconds!

The girl bees in the hive are the true workers who handle all the important jobs. They are strong and hardworking, and they are in charge of building the hive, cleaning it, and feeding the baby bees.

Most importantly, they are the ones responsible for making honey. When they gather the sugary liquid from flowers, called nectar, they store it in their honey stomach and transform it into honey.

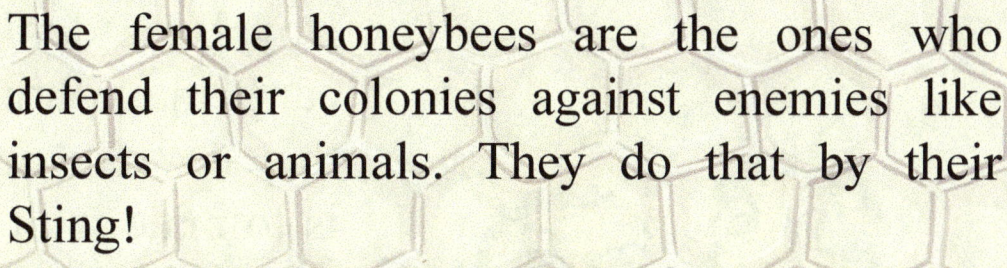

The female honeybees are the ones who defend their colonies against enemies like insects or animals. They do that by their Sting!

A bee sting is both fascinating and painful! It's how bees defend themselves and their hive when they feel threatened. They sting with their stinger, which is why getting close to a honeybee hive can be dangerous without protection. The honeybees might think you are an enemy and could attack and sting you.

A honeybee can sting only once because its stinger gets stuck in the victim, and the bee will die shortly afterward. The bee's sting releases a small amount of venom, which can trigger an allergic reaction. This is why it hurts and burns, and it may cause swelling or more severe reactions that might require medical attention.

**What about the Boy bees? They are called the Drone Bees.**

Boy Bees don't sting, and they can't make honey. So, what do they do? The male bee's only job is to mate with the queen bee so she can lay eggs. They travel from colony to colony, and that's why they are called drone bees. Their sole purpose is to mate with a queen from another hive to help make new bee babies. Sadly, they don't live much longer after that. So maybe they don't have it that easy after all!

**Why Are Honey Bees Important?**
Bees don't just make honey; they also help plants grow by transferring pollen from flower to flower. This process is called pollination, and without it, we wouldn't have many of the fruits and vegetables we love, like apples, strawberries, and even cocoa trees that make chocolate! Imagine a world without chocolate—no way, right?

Honey isn't just sweet and delicious; it's also packed with benefits! It is full of nutrients like vitamins, minerals, and antioxidants that help keep you healthy. Honey can soothe a sore throat and even help your skin in healing and staying healthy.

Fun fact: Honey never goes bad! Archaeologists have discovered honey in ancient Egyptian tombs that are still safe to eat, even thousands of years later!

Beekeepers are people who take care of bees and collect their honey. They wear special protective suits to avoid stings while working with the hives. Thank you, beekeepers, for your amazing work collecting honey and helping the bees!

# Great Wall of China

Have you ever heard about The Great Wall of China?

In northern China lies a huge ancient wall stretching for 13,000 miles (21000 kilometers) . It's so big that If you tried to walk the entire length, it would take a whole year. This is the Great Wall of China.

It stands 20-26 feet high ( 6-8 meters ) , and it is 13 to 16 feet wide (4 to 5 meters), wide enough for soldiers, horses, and even wagons to travel along the top.

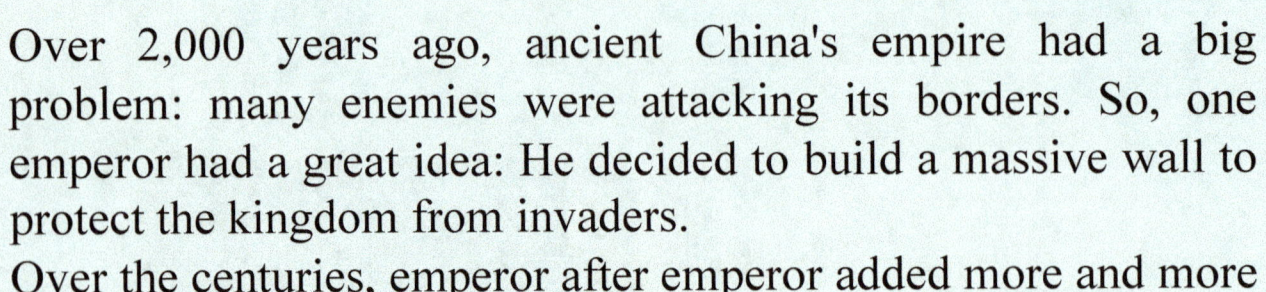

Over 2,000 years ago, ancient China's empire had a big problem: many enemies were attacking its borders. So, one emperor had a great idea: He decided to build a massive wall to protect the kingdom from invaders.

Over the centuries, emperor after emperor added more and more segments to the wall, making it even stronger and longer.

Eventually, these additions came together to form what we now call the Great Wall of China, a true marvel of human engineering and determination!

**What Was It Made Of?**
Builders used materials like stone, bricks, and wood. In some sections of the wall built during the Ming Dynasty, a unique mortar was used—made from lime and sticky rice! Yes, that's right, they used rice to help stick the bricks together.

Today, the Great Wall of China is still one of the world's most famous and iconic structures. Millions of people visit each year to enjoy the breathtaking views and take pictures, imagining the soldiers who once guarded the kingdom thousands of years ago.

# Albert Einstein

Alright, kiddos! Let me tell you about one of the most brilliant minds in history—**Albert Einstein**!

Einstein was like a superhero of science, and his superpower was thinking about the universe in ways no one ever had before! He's famous not only for his wild hair but also for his **Theory of Relativity**. Einstein was fascinated by understanding the mysteries of space and time. Albert Einstein was born in 1879 in Germany. He moved to America and died there in 1955. And guess what? When he was a kid, he didn't talk very much, and some people thought he wasn't that smart! Crazy, right? But little did they know, his brain was working in ways that would change the world forever.

Einstein was fascinated by light—yes, the same light that comes from a flashlight or the Sun. Light travels very, very fast! In fact, light is the fastest thing we know, moving at about 300,000 kilometers per second (or 186,000 miles per second). To grasp how fast that is, light can go around the Earth 7 and a half times in just one second—that's super fast!

Einstein discovered that things that move really, really fast experience time more slowly compared to someone who isn't moving as fast. So if a spaceship could travel close to the speed of light, time inside that spaceship would slow down compared to time on Earth.

## Time Dilation

Einstein's imagination was so powerful that he could picture how the universe works in ways no one had before. He realized that when something moves extremely fast, time slows down for it. This strange effect is known as Time Dilation.

Why Time is Different in Space when you move really fast! Imagine you have two friends: Ryan and George. George stays on Earth, but Ryan goes on a superfast spaceship to explore space. Ryan's spaceship is so fast that it's almost traveling at the speed of light, which is the fastest thing in the universe!

**Ryan**
Going on space trip

**George**
Staying on Earth

Now, here's where it gets cool: because Ryan is moving so fast in space, time starts to slow down for him compared to George, who is still on Earth. So one minute for Ryan would be many days for George.

Meanwhile, a lot more time is passed for George on Earth! As his time is still normal not slowing down

So when Ryan returns after a short trip, he finds out that years have gone by on Earth! George on earth might have grown older, but Ryan has hardly aged at all. It's like time traveled slower for him because he was going so fast in space.

So, the faster you travel through space, the slower time moves for you compared to people who are not moving as fast; this is called **Time Dilation**! That was one of the amazing discoveries that Einstein made !

# Dinosaurs

Dinosaurs were big, scaly creatures; they lived on Earth millions of years ago. They dominated the planet for a long time but disappeared around 65 million years ago.

Dinosaurs roamed the Earth long before any humans existed. Humans have been around for only a few hundred thousand years, which is a brief period compared to the vast history of our planet. Some dinosaurs were enormous, like Tyrannosaurus Rex (T-Rex), the king of the dinosaurs! With its massive head, sharp teeth, and tiny arms.

# Brachiosaurus

*pronounced like this:*
*BRACK-ee-oh-SAW-rus*

The **Brachiosaurus** is one of the most iconic dinosaurs, known for its long neck and massive size. Brachiosaurus was incredibly tall, standing about 40–50 feet (12–15 meters) high! And weighed as much as 40–80 tons, about the same as 10–15 elephants combined!

During the Late Jurassic Period, Brachiosaurus roamed the Earth around 150 million years ago. It lived in what is now North America, and fossils have been found in the United States, particularly in Colorado and Utah.

Despite its massive size, the Brachiosaurus was a herbivore, which means it only ate plants. Its lengthy neck enabled it to reach high into trees to nibble on leaves.

For such a massive dinosaur, Brachiosaurus had a surprisingly small brain. Its brain was about the size of a human fist, which is tiny compared to its enormous body. Despite this, it was well-adapted to its environment and thrived for millions of years. Brachiosaurus was a peaceful giant that ruled the forests of the Jurassic period, towering over other dinosaurs and reaching heights no other land animal could attain!

# Velociraptors ( the Raptors )

Were smaller-sized dinosaurs compared to the other dinosaurs at that time. Still, their small size didn't make them any less dangerous! **Velociraptors** had a large, curved claw on each foot, often referred to as a "killing claw. It is believed that Velociraptors were smart, as they had relatively large brains compared to their body size; Velociraptors are thought to have been highly intelligent for dinosaurs.

**Stegosaurus**, on the other hand, had small brains, the size of a walnut! Stegosaurus were as big as a bus; they had big plates on their backs and spiky tails for defense. No one messed with Stegosaurus unless they wanted a good smack!

Some Dinosaurs had a body with Armor like Ankylosaurus; they were like walking tanks! They had armor plates covering their backs, and they even had big, club-like tails to swing at any predator trying to snack on them.

The **Triceratops** had three big horns on its head and a huge bony frill at the back of its head. If a T. Rex came looking for trouble, the Triceratops would lower its head, show those sharp horns, and charge just like a dinosaur bulldozer! Triceratops were also herbivores who only munched on plants and fruits all-day

Not all dinosaurs were stomping around on the ground like T. Rex; some soared through the skies, while others swam in the water!

Flying Dinos: These guys are called **Pterosaurs**! They soared through the skies with huge wings, looking like giant bats. **Pterodactyl** is a famous one, and it had a long, pointy beak. They likely fed on fish and small marine creatures by swooping down over the water and snatching prey with their beaks.

Swimming Dinos: they were the underwater kings! Although they weren't technically dinosaurs, they existed during the same period. Plesiosaurs had long necks and flippers, resembling a blend of a dolphin and a giraffe. They glided through the water hunting for fish.

# Extinction : The Big Goodbye

What is extinction? Extinction occurs when every individual of a species, such as dinosaurs, is gone forever. Dinosaurs went extinct about 65 million years ago during a massive event known as the K-Pg event.

It happened because a huge space rock (an asteroid struck Earth, resulting in an enormous explosion, larger than anything imaginable! This triggered widespread fires, and the resulting smoke and dust blocked out sunlight, plunging everything into cold and darkness. Trees began to die, making it extremely difficult for dinosaurs to find food or stay warm. Unfortunately, this marked the end of the dinosaurs' reign on Earth.

# The Oxygen

Oxygen is one of the secrets of life! Oxygen is a part of the air we breathe. Even though you can't see or smell it, it's all around us! Every time you breathe, your body gets a fresh gulp of oxygen.

Think of oxygen as the fuel your body needs to keep running and moving. When you breathe in, your lungs pull in oxygen from the air, and your blood carries it to every part of your body, including your brain, heart, muscles, and even your toes!

Oxygen is super important for all living things—we simply can't live without it! It's everywhere in the air, and it's one of the many reasons why planet Earth is habitable

There is no oxygen to breathe in space, on Mars, or on the Moon. That's why astronauts use oxygen tanks on the back of their space suits to give them the air they need to breathe.

The same thing happens when people dive into the ocean, they carry oxygen tanks on their backs because humans cannot breathe underwater.

But wait, I thought all animals needed oxygen. So how come can fish breathe underwater?

Well, the ocean and seawater have oxygen dissolved in them. Fish have a special organ called *gills*. These gills allow the fish to extract oxygen from the water. As fish push water into their mouths, it passes through the gills, pulling out the oxygen they need to survive!

Oxygen helps the body turn food into energy. After oxygen helps produce energy, there is some leftover waste that your body no longer needs. This waste is known as **Carbon Dioxide or $CO_2$**. Think of it like the trash left after a big party: your organs don't want it, so they need to dispose of it!

# Carbon Dioxide ($CO_2$)

The $CO_2$ leaves our body through the mouth and nose when we exhale. So, when we breathe in, we take in oxygen from the air (**inhale**) into our lungs, and when we breathe out, our lungs get rid of the waste $CO_2$ by **exhaling**.

**Inhale:** the lungs fill up with Oxygen

**Exhale:** the lung push out the carbon dioxide CO2

Let me tell you a little secret about $CO_2$. Unlike good ol' oxygen, our bodies can't use $CO_2$ to make energy; nope! In fact, if too much $CO_2$ hangs around us, it can be pretty harmful. Yikes!

And guess what? It's not just us breathing out that produces $CO_2$. Oh no, there's much more! A whole lot of $CO_2$ comes from burning fuels like coal, oil, and natural gas. And where does all this burning happen? Well, it mainly occurs in factories that manufacture products and generate electricity. Plus, $CO_2$ comes from burning gas to heat our homes. And don't forget, it also comes from the engines of cars and airplanes! That's why we need to monitor how much we burn, so we can keep our planet nice and cool!

# Photosynthesis!

So what happens to all that **CO₂** floating around in the air?

Believe it or not, trees and other plants work magic just like wizards, taking in CO₂ (carbon dioxide) to make their own food—amazing, right?

Here's how their magic works: Trees take water from the soil and mix it with carbon dioxide from the air. Then, with a little help from sunlight, they whip up something yummy for themselves called sugar!

And while trees make their delicious sugar, they give us an amazing gift: **Oxygen**! How kind of them, huh?

Trees, green grass, and ocean plants act like massive oxygen factories, constantly absorbing carbon dioxide, mixing it with water, and using sunlight to produce more and more oxygen. This remarkable process is called photosynthesis! That's why it's super important to protect our trees and forests to keep our oxygen factory working and the Earth healthy and happy!

# The Octopus

These underwater creatures are truly unique. Not only do they have eight legs, but they also have three hearts! Yes, octopuses have three hearts! Two pump blood to their gills, while one pumps it to the rest of their body. When they swim, the heart that pumps blood to their body stops, which is why they prefer crawling!

Unlike us, octopuses have **blue blood** because they contain copper, not iron like ours. Blue blood helps them survive in deep, low-oxygen waters

Octopuses are among the smartest animals in the ocean! They can solve puzzles and change their color and texture to blend into their surroundings, making them just like underwater ninjas!

# Africa

Let's talk about the amazing continent of **Africa!**

Africa is a continent full of vibrant cultures, rich history, and incredible natural beauty. It is the second-largest continent, home to 54 diverse countries that range from lush rainforests and vast deserts to rolling savannas and bustling cities. Africa is also the birthplace of human civilization!

Africa is the home to ancient landmarks like the Great Pyramids of Egypt!

Samburu

Zulu

Till these days, many traditional tribes still follow ancient customs, From the colorful Samburu tribes in Kenya, who travel around with their sheep and cows, to the Zulu tribe of South Africa, who are Known for their history of great warriors and vibrant cultural ceremonies, especially their dances and beautiful beadwork.

# Africa wild Life!

**Africa** is truly the **kingdom of wildlife**! It's famous for some of the most incredible animals on the planet.

Lions, known as the "King of the Jungle," roam the savannas. Elephants, specifically the African elephant, are the largest land animals on Earth, equipped with massive ears that help them stay cool under the hot African sun. Giraffes, with their long necks and incredibly long tongues, and zebras, which have unique black and white stripes, each zebra's stripes are as distinctive as human fingerprints!

Cheetahs are the fastest land animals on Earth. While hyenas may appear as if they're always laughing, they are serious hunters with powerful teeth and jaws. Rhinos are massive creatures known for their horns and tough skin. Gorillas inhabit the dense jungles of Central Africa, where you'll find them as the largest primates on Earth! They live in family groups called troops and spend most of their time eating fruits and leaves.

# The Sahara Desert

The natural wonders of Africa are truly fascinating! Africa is home to the world's largest desert, the Sahara, which is located in northern Africa and covers an area greater than the entire United States of America. It is a captivating place full of sand dunes, known for its blazing daytime heat; during the day, the Sahara can be one of the hottest places on Earth, and at night, it can reach freezing temperatures.

Despite its harsh conditions, the Sahara is home to a variety of plants and animals that have adapted to the tough environment, such as the fennec fox and the dromedary camel.

The Dromedary camel (Arabian Camel), also known as the "Ship of the Desert," is built for survival in the harsh conditions of the Sahara. It can go for days or even weeks without water and can drink up to 40 gallons in one go. Unlike the Mongolian camel with two humps, the dromedary has one hump filled with fat, not water, which gives it energy when food and water are scarce.

The Fennec Fox is an adorable, small fox that lives in the Sahara Desert! It's the smallest fox in the world, but even though it's small, it has huge ears! These big ears help the Fennec Fox stay cool by releasing heat, and they also allow the fox to hear even the tiniest movements under the sand. They are nocturnal, which means they are most active at night when it's cooler.

Not only have animals adapted to the harsh Sahara Desert, but so have people, namely, the tribes known as the **Berber** and **Tuareg**.

Let me introduce you to some amazing people from the Sahara desert and mountains of North Africa, **the Berbers**! Or, as they like to call themselves, the Amazigh, which means "free people"!

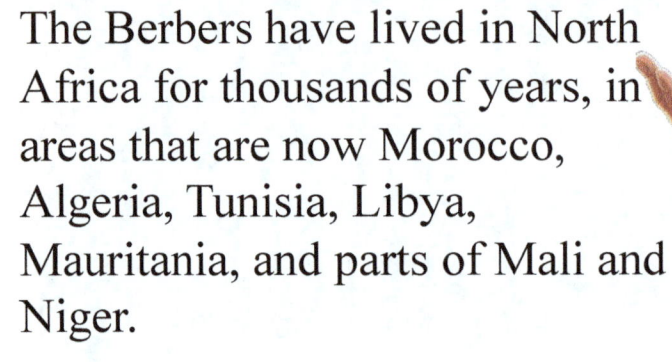

The Berbers have lived in North Africa for thousands of years, in areas that are now Morocco, Algeria, Tunisia, Libya, Mauritania, and parts of Mali and Niger.

Berbers thrive in tough environments, from the super-hot Sahara Desert to the cold high mountains. They wear colorful robes, often in white and blue, and craft beautiful jewelry. Like the Tuareg tribe, which is part of the Berber family, they travel across the desert on camels. Berbers are experts at surviving in the desert with very little water and navigating the vast Sahara.

# The Berbers

# King Mansa Musa

One of the most fascinating stories in African history is the tale of **the richest man in history, King Mansa Musa**.

Mansa Musa was the king of the Mali Empire in West Africa during the 14th century, and his wealth was legendary. He ruled the Mali Empire from 1312 to 1337. Under his leadership, the empire became rich and powerful due to its vast resources of gold and salt. The Mali Empire was one of the largest in West Africa, controlling important trade routes across the Sahara Desert.

One of the most famous stories about Mansa Musa is his pilgrimage to Mecca (known as a hajj in Islam) in 1324. He didn't travel alone, he brought a massive caravan of 60,000 people and carried tons of gold. Along the way, he distributed so much gold that it sparked myths about cities built entirely of gold in Africa!

# Archimedes

Over 2,200 years ago, a king received a beautiful new golden crown in Ancient Greece. However, the king became suspicious that the crown might not be made of pure gold and could be mixed with cheaper metals. He wanted to know the truth but didn't want to damage or break the crown to find out. He did not know how !?

The king called for one of the brightest mathematicians of the time and asked him to figure out whether the crown was made of pure gold or mixed with other metals—without damaging it. And that brilliant young man was none other than **Archimedes!**

Archimedes was no ordinary young man. He was incredibly smart and always curious about the world around him. As a result, he became one of the most famous Greek mathematicians, astronomers, and inventors.

But back when the king gave him the golden crown puzzle, he didn't know how to solve it right away. He had no idea!

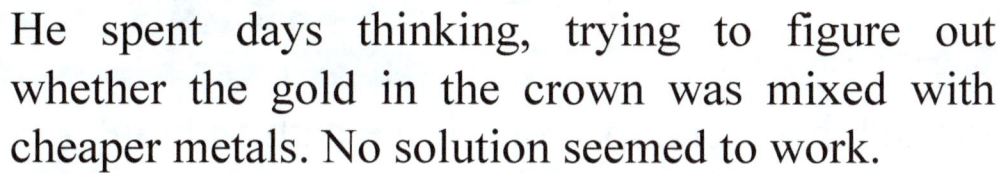

He spent days thinking, trying to figure out whether the gold in the crown was mixed with cheaper metals. No solution seemed to work.

Then, one day, Archimedes was taking a bath in an ancient Greek bathtub. As he stepped into the tub, which was filled to the brim with water, he noticed that water spilled over the edge when he got in. At that moment, it hit him—he had figured out the crown puzzle!

Archimedes was so excited that he jumped out of the bath and ran through the streets shouting, "Eureka! Eureka!" which means, "I've found it! I've found it!"

And from that moment on, it's been called the **Eureka moment!** Every time scientists or someone makes an amazing discovery, they shout, "Eureka!" to celebrate their big breakthrough.

One day, you will have your very own Eureka moment, my friend, when you make a splendid new discovery!

But what did he actually discover?

> To understand how **Archimedes** solved the puzzle, let's explore this scenario.

If you have 1 kilogram ( or 2.2 pounds ) of iron and compare it to 1 kilogram of wood, the wood will need to be much larger in size (have a bigger volume) to weigh the same as the iron.

Now, even though both objects weigh the same, if you place them in a water container, the wood will displace much more water out than the iron because they are made of different materials, and the 1 kilogram of wood is much larger in size than the 1 kilogram of iron. This difference in density means the wood takes up more space and pushes out more water than the iron

Archimedes realized that when any object is submerged in water, it displaces an amount of water equal to its volume. This means the more space an object takes up, the more water it pushes out.

This is how Archimedes was able to tell the king whether the crown was made of pure gold. They brought a piece of pure gold that weighed the same as the crown.
then placed both the gold and the crown in water-filled containers to measure how much water each would displace.

If both were made of pure gold, they would displace the same amount of water. However, if the crown displaced more or less water, it meant that the crown was mixed with other materials.

To the king's surprise, the crown displaced more water than the lump of pure gold, proving that it wasn't made of pure gold. The goldsmith likely mixed in a lighter metal to deceive the king! The goldsmith was in serious trouble, but Archimedes became one of the king's favorite advisors for solving the puzzle.

# Buoyancy!

Archimedes didn't just help the king—he helped all of humanity in understanding something incredibly important. His discovery clarified how objects float on water! Have you ever wondered why a small rock sinks to the ocean floor while a massive ship floats? Well, the answer is what we call buoyancy!

So, what is **Buoyanc**y?
It means when you push the water away, it pushes you back up.

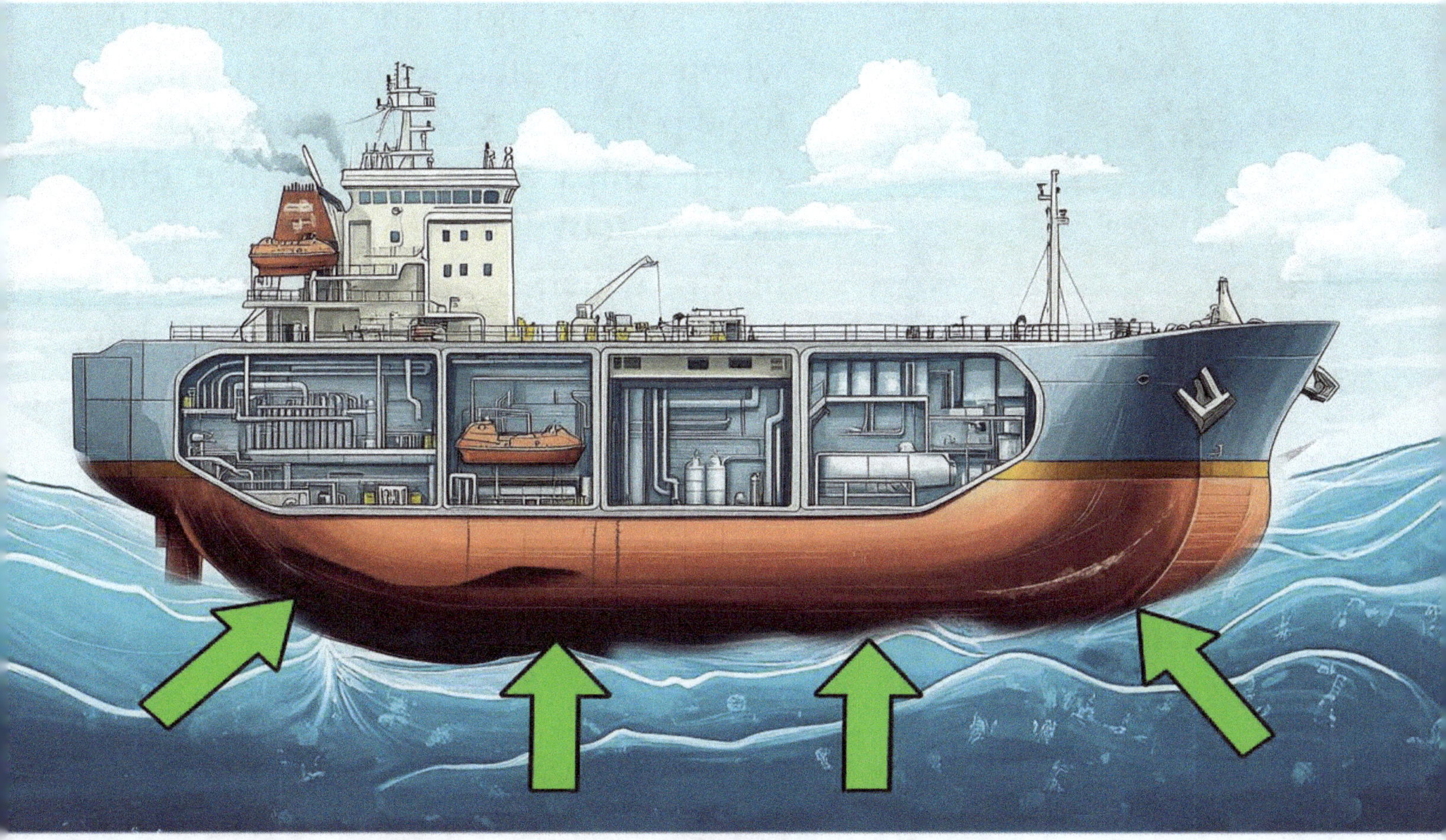

When a huge ship enters the water, it pushes a big amount of water out of the way, and all that displaced water says, "Hey, ship! I'm going to push you back up!" The more water the ship pushes out of the way, the harder the water pushes back, lifting the ship. That's why ships float!

Now, what about the poor little rock?

Well, rocks don't push enough water away, and they're very dense (which means they're heavy for their size). The water just can't push the rock back up, so down it goes. Poor rock!

**And here's another fun fact:**

Air is very light and doesn't sink, which is why floaties are filled with air to help them stay on the surface of the water. Ships are somewhat like giant floaties too! They're filled with air inside, which makes them less dense than the water, so they float like champions! But rocks? They're full of rocky stuff—heavy, dense rocky stuff—and that's why the water can't hold them.

**So next time you see a ship on the water, you'll know: it's all about buoyancy, air, and some very cool Archimedes effect!**

# The Age of Discovery

Have you ever tasted food that got so much better with a sprinkle of pepper or a dash of cinnamon? Those magical ingredients are known as spices, and they really do make food delicious! But the story of spices goes far beyond just tasty meals, spices have shaped history and changed the world!

A long time ago in Europe, food wasn't all that tasty, it was pretty plain because there were no spices to add flavor! Plus, food would spoil quickly without refrigerators and sometimes develop a bad smell. Spices helped preserve food and cover up those unpleasant odors, so getting spices became very important to make meals delicious and safe!

# The Age of Discovery

Spices weren't the only treasures that Europeans loved from Asia and China! For clothing, Europeans were used to rough fabrics like wool and linen. But silk? Silk was like magic! It was soft and smooth and had a shiny, luxurious look that enchanted everyone. Europeans couldn't get enough of its elegance and beauty!

Spices, silk, gold, and jewelry, these were treasures that Europe craved and were abundant in Asia! But in those days, getting these goods wasn't easy or safe. Traveling between countries and continents was a long, dangerous journey.

# The Silk Road

These treasures traveled across a long, dusty route called the **Silk Road**, connecting Europe to Asia through the Middle East. But this journey was no walk in the park! It was long took months to a year, and it was dangerous, and costly, with local rulers and empires charging taxes and tolls along the way. Plus, conflicts in the Middle East often made things even tougher for traders!

European kings and lords sought new ways to access the valuable goods and treasures of Asia; They looked to the sea as a potential route to reach these distant lands to avoid the dangerous, expensive land Silk Road.

At that time, Portugal was a powerful kingdom in Europe. The Portuguese began sending ships into the unknown waters of the Atlantic, hoping to find a way around Africa. Finally, in 1498, Portuguese explorer **Vasco da Gama** achieved a historic breakthrough by sailing around the southern tip of Africa, known as the **Cape of Good Hope**. He successfully reached India!

His trip opened a new sea route between Europe and the Indian Ocean. This achievement sparked a wave of sea exploration and intensified trade between Europe and Asia.

# Christopher Columbus

The success achieved by the Portuguese king did not sit well with their neighbor, the Spanish Kingdom. King Ferdinand II and his wife, Queen Isabella, wanted to compete with Portugal in exploring new routes to India and Asia to build wealth. They needed a clever plan, but no one had any brilliant ideas... until one day, an Italian sailor with a bit of a wild look in his eye showed up. This was Christopher Columbus!

**He came to the Queen Isabella and her King with the craziest idea!**

"Your Majesties," he said, "why not sail west to reach India? I believe the world is round, and if we go this way, we'll get there even faster than the Portuguese!"

After obtaining support from the King and the Queen of Spain, Columbus set sail from Spain in the summer of 1492, with three ships Niña , Pinta , The Santa María, Columbus headed west where no man has gone before , or that what he thought!

As the days stretched on with no sight of land, their food and fresh water supplies dwindled.

Many of Columbus's sailors were terrified of venturing into the unknown. They feared sea monsters and believed they might sail off the edge of the Earth.

After five long weeks at sea, the sailors began to see seagulls flying over the ship, signaling they were getting close to land. Finally, Christopher Columbus reached his destination, or so he thought! He believed he had arrived in India. However, he had actually landed on what is known today as the Bahamas, part of the Americas.

Columbus didn't realize he had discovered a "New World." When he met the Indigenous people there, they were welcoming and kind to him and his crew. They exchanged food, water, and gifts, marking the start of a historic encounter.

Columbus made several trips back and forth along his newly discovered route, believing he had found a path to Asia. However, a few years later, another Italian explorer, **Amerigo Vespucci,** traveled the same route and realized something extraordinary: they were not in Asia at all! Vespucci concluded that they had actually discovered an entirely new continent.

Vespucci was the first to create a map showing this "New World" as a separate landmass, distinct from Asia. In honor of his insight, the continent was named **"America"** after him, recognizing his role in identifying it as a new part of the world.

This was just the beginning of a new era, a time of European exploration in the New World that would change the course of history for Europe and the Americas forever.

With each new voyage, explorers sought riches, treasures, and tales of legendary cities made of gold! However, sadly, this was not just a story of excitement and discovery.

The Native peoples, who had lived in the Americas for thousands of years, faced a harsh reality. Constant waves of European expeditions brought great suffering to their lives as explorers claimed land, searched for fortunes, and changed the world around them. But don't worry, that's a story for another day, my friends!

# Social Skills

Let's talk a little bit about social skills. What are they, you might ask? Well, they're the art of making friends! And anyone can learn these skills.

Social skills are the art of interacting with people. They're how we act, talk, and listen around others. Think of them as magic tools that help you make new friends, understand how others feel, work together with others, and solve problems in a kind way

**When you meet someone new:** People love a warm smile! So, when you meet someone, look them in the eye, smile, and say hi. Tell them your name and ask for theirs. Remember: **SMILE, HI, 'My name is [your name]. What's your name?**

**Be a good listener means not just hearing someone but paying attention to what they say;** when your friend tells you a story, listen carefully and show them you care. Ask them questions about it to show you're interested and make them feel special

**Listening makes people feel heard and happy!**

**Be kind to people:** Kindness is like sunshine; it makes everyone feel warm! Help your friend if they're in trouble, like if they trip off their bike. Give compliments when they do something nice, like saying, 'That's a great drawing!

Take turns when you play with others. This shows that you are patient, care about others, and are a fair person!

Look people in the eye when you talk to them. It shows you're interested and paying attention!
( EYE CONTACT) is a very important

Sometimes, we make mistakes, oops! But saying, "I'm sorry," helps fix things. Forgiving others shows you're kind and understanding.

**Practice Makes Perfect** Social skills are like muscles; you get better by practicing! Start with small steps, like smiling at someone new or sharing a toy. Before you know it, you'll be a social skills superstar

# Message to Aliens!

Well, kiddos, back in the groovy year of 1977, the brilliant scientists at NASA had a wild idea! They thought, "Hey, what if we sent a message to aliens?" Yup, that's right, Aliens!

So, they decided to launch a spacecraft carrying a message for extraterrestrial life. But wait a second… do we even know where the aliens are? Hmm, not really! So how on Earth, or space, I should say, did they plan to pull that off? Let's dive into this cosmic story of Voyager 1 and Voyager 2 space crafts!

So, NASA built not one, but TWO spacecraft, Voyager 1 and Voyager 2! Their mission? To explore the outer planets of our solar system and then head off into the space between the stars, interstellar space! And guess what? They even packed a message for aliens on board these twin spacecrafts in case anyone out there is listening!

The two twin spacecraft, Voyager 1 and Voyager 2, were launched one month apart in 1977. They traveled through our solar system, collecting incredible information and stunning images as they flew by the giant planets Jupiter and Saturn while also making groundbreaking discoveries about their moons.

Voyager 1 discovered active volcanoes on Io, one of Jupiter's moons, and identified a thick atmosphere on Titan, Saturn's largest moon. In 2012, Voyager 1 became the first spacecraft to leave the solar system, entering the space between the stars (interstellar space).

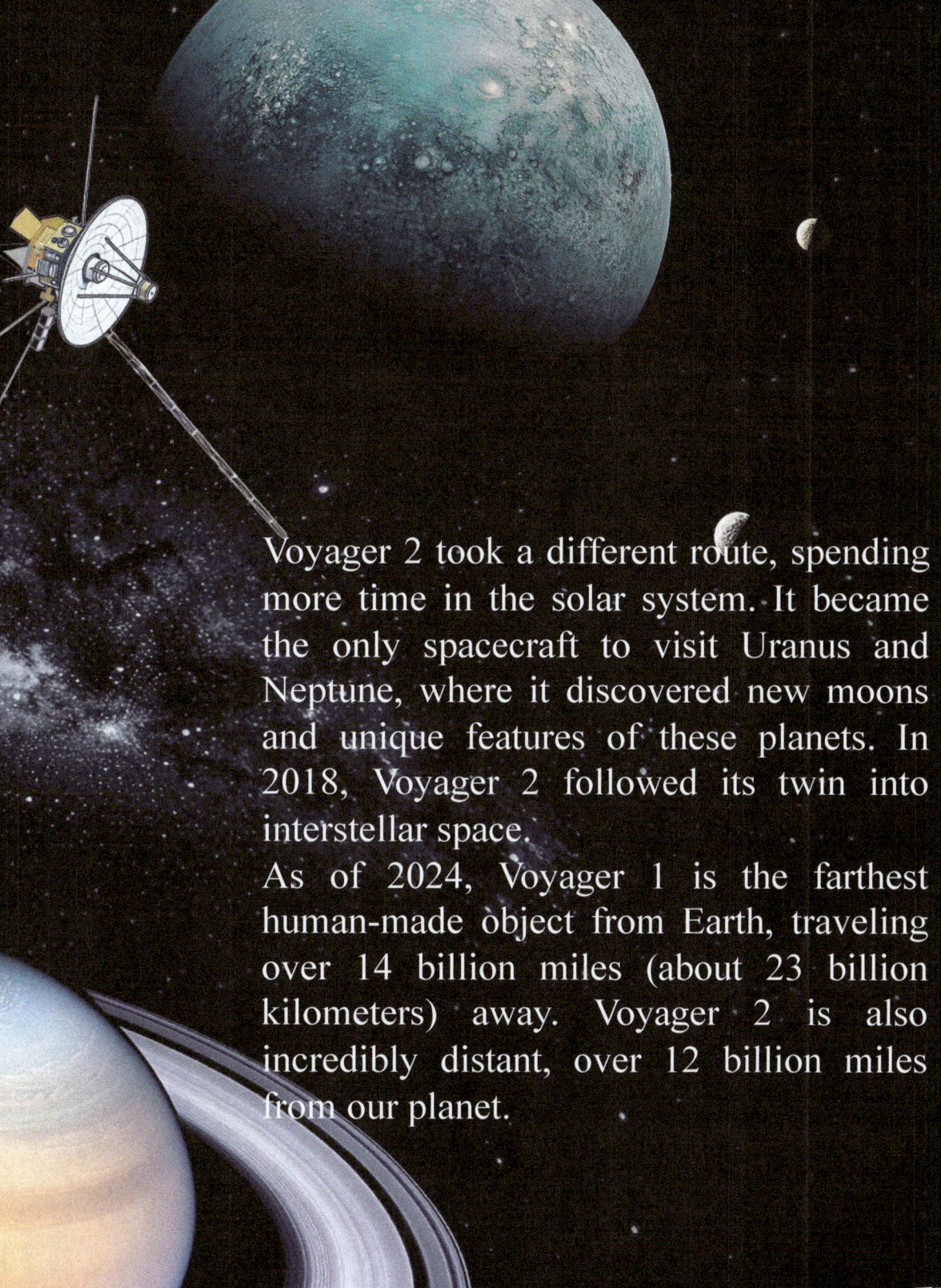

Voyager 2 took a different route, spending more time in the solar system. It became the only spacecraft to visit Uranus and Neptune, where it discovered new moons and unique features of these planets. In 2018, Voyager 2 followed its twin into interstellar space.

As of 2024, Voyager 1 is the farthest human-made object from Earth, traveling over 14 billion miles (about 23 billion kilometers) away. Voyager 2 is also incredibly distant, over 12 billion miles from our planet.

Since these two spacecraft were destined to leave the solar system and venture into the unknown depths of space, scientists wanted to send a message with them—a message that could be found millions or even billions of years from now by anyone or anything in the vast cosmos.

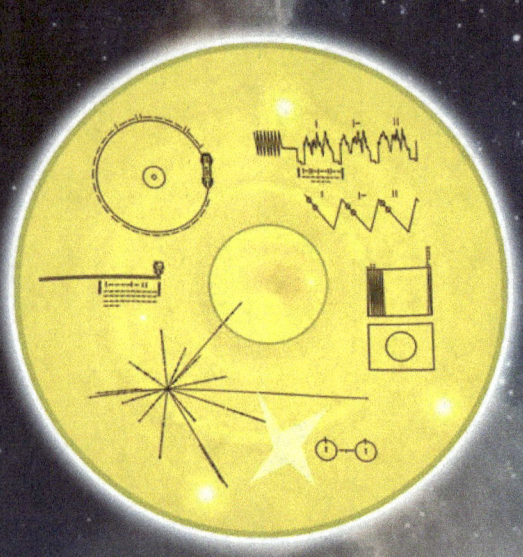

This message would capture the essence of human civilization and the story of life on our tiny planet, Earth. They're like time capsules, floating through the stars.
The scientists placed this message on a **golden plate** called the **Golden Record**. This record is like a cosmic puzzle for any intelligent aliens to solve. If they figure it out, they can unlock a treasure trove of Earth's wonders!

This golden record has Sounds of Earth: Birds, ocean waves, and even music and songs. Aliens would be Greeted with "Hello " in 55 languages; the golden record also has Photos of Earth showing people smiling, working, and living their lives, along with images of animals, mountains, and oceans. Most of all, a map of our location points to where Earth is in the galaxy so the aliens know where this spacecraft came from.

Voyager wasn't the only spacecraft sent with a message to aliens? Nope! A few years earlier, NASA launched two other brave adventurers into the cosmos: Pioneer 10 and Pioneer 11. These two space scouts were sent to explore the outer planets, and they also carried a golden plate. This plate had pictures of humans and planet Earth, along with a star map to show where we live in the galaxy!

If there really are intelligent aliens out there, and if they can decode the instructions on how to play these messages, they'll get a sneak peek into what life was like on Earth at the time the Voyager and Pioneer spacecraft were built. These golden messages could last for billions of years, carrying the story of our civilization into eternity.

# The story of Money

Have you ever used money? Did you notice that every time you buy something from a store or grab food at a restaurant, you must pay with money? But have you ever wondered why that is? And how did money even come to exist in the first place?

Money is important for everyone. People work hard to earn and save it. So, Let's dive into the fascinating story of how money came to be!

A long time ago, people had no concept of money. Instead, they hunted animals and grew plants to gather food and make clothes. But as time went on, some people became better at certain skills—like hunting, crafting, or farming- than others.

For example, hunters would trade food in exchange for beautifully crafted clothes made from animal fur. People began exchanging goods and services to get what they needed, and this trading system was called **Bartering**. It was the first step toward creating an economy!

Bartering worked well for a while, but eventually, problems began to arise. What if you needed food, but the food seller didn't need your service? You would have to offer something else of value to make the trade. To solve this, people began choosing specific items that everyone agreed had value. At first, they used things like seashells, shiny rocks, or beads as a way to buy goods.

Even in ancient times, salt was incredibly important! It was so valuable in Ancient Egypt and Rome that Roman soldiers used salt to trade goods among themselves. In fact, the Roman soldiers received an allowance of salt called **"Salarium,"** which is where the word **"Salary"** comes from. Yes, salt was like gold back then!

People quickly became fascinated by the beauty of shiny gold and silver. They started using gold nuggets, flakes, and even pieces of silver to trade for goods and services. These precious metals were among the earliest forms of money "currency."

Then came the invention of coins! The first known coins were created in the ancient **Kingdom of Lydia**, which thrived in modern-day Turkey. Around **600 BCE**, during the reign of **King Alyattes**, the Lydians minted the first metal coins. These coins were made of **Electrum**, a naturally occurring mix of gold and silver, and were stamped with designs like lions.

Once Lydia introduced them, every kingdom wanted in on the action. They started making their own coins, each stamped with unique designs to show off their royal flair. Why were coins such a hit? Well, for starters, they were tough little guys, no breaking or crumbling like shells or beads. They were easy to carry around, And best of all, coins made shopping so much simpler. For the first time, people had a clear idea of how much things cost!

Carrying coins was fine for a while, for a few hundred years in fact, but imagine your pockets sagging with all that metal! Then, in the 7th century, the brilliant minds of ancient China had a *eureka moment*! They thought, 'Why carry the actual treasure when we can use something lighter to represent it?' And thus, paper money was born! The paper money ( the paper Currency or bills ) had different values tied to actual treasure, gold, and silver, stored safely elsewhere. Genius, right?

Soon, the idea spread like wildfire, and every country started making its own versions of this magical paper money ( currency )!

Money bills are decorated with intricate designs, secret inks, and hidden stamps. Why? To outsmart the tricksters who might dare to make fake copies ( counterfeit ) of their beautiful currency!

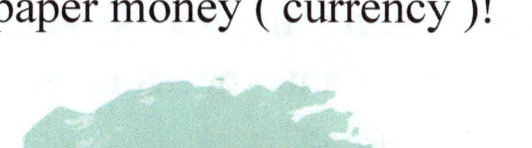

Now, brace yourselves, kids, because the newest form of money will blow your socks off! This money isn't made of paper, metal, or anything you can touch. Nope! It's invisible and mysterious, so hidden, in fact, that we call it Crypto-Currency (which means Hidden Money).

So what is it? It's money created on computers using some of the most complicated math you can imagine. It doesn't live in your piggy bank or wallet; it lives on a super-smart, magical system called the **Blockchain**, a giant network of computers spread all over the planet.

What makes it even cooler? This cryptocurrency doesn't exist in real life; it's like a video game coin! The most famous of these is **Bitcoin**.

People around the world are starting to use cryptocurrencies more and more. You can use them to buy things, trade for services, or even store your regular money in the form of crypto.

And who knows? Maybe one day, you'll be buying ice cream with Bitcoin or even inventing the next big cryptocurrency yourself!

# Alexander the Great

Over 2,000 years ago, in the kingdom of Macedonia ( where Greece is located today ), a wise man created a knot from a rope called **"the Gordian Knot"** that was so complicated that no one could untie it. According to legend, a man would one day come and solve the Gordian knot and be destined to rule the world.

A young king in his twenties, who had just inherited the throne, wasted no time solving the legendary knot. Determined to prove he was the man destined to rule the world, he believed the prophecy spoke of him. Without hesitation, he drew his sword and split the Gordian Knot into pieces.

This young king was none other than Alexander the Great, who went on to rule vast regions of the known world during his era.

When Alexander was a young child, both he and his father, the King at the time, believed that knowledge was the greatest power a man could have. Alexander wanted to be the smartest kid alive and was eager to learn everything. To help him achieve this, his father hired one of the most famous philosophers of all time, **Aristotle**. Under Aristotle's guidance, Alexander learned about science, history, and philosophy. This wealth of knowledge helped Alexander grow into a wise and capable leader, becoming a great king at a remarkably young age.

Alexander's horse, **Bucephalus**, was a **black** horse with a white star on its forehead. Bucephalus was considered wild and untamable until young Alexander figured out that the horse was afraid of its own shadow. By turning the horse toward the sun so it couldn't see its shadow, Alexander was able to calm and ride it. They had a bond, and Bucephalus became legendary, and the horse accompanied Alexander in many battles

So, why do people call Alexander of Macedonia "Alexander the Great"? When Alexander was only 20 years old, his father was killed, and he became the new king. He was a very ambitious young ruler and decided to expand his kingdom. He began by conquering Greece. Then, he moved east toward the powerful Persian Empire. At that time, Persia was ruled by King Darius III, but Alexander defeated him and took over the empire.

After that, Alexander turned west and conquered Egypt, where he founded the famous city of Alexandria. Not stopping there, he marched further east toward India. However, his army faced a tough challenge: Indian war elephants! Although Alexander did not lose the battle, his army was exhausted, so he turned back and allowed the Indian king to continue ruling his kingdom.

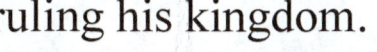
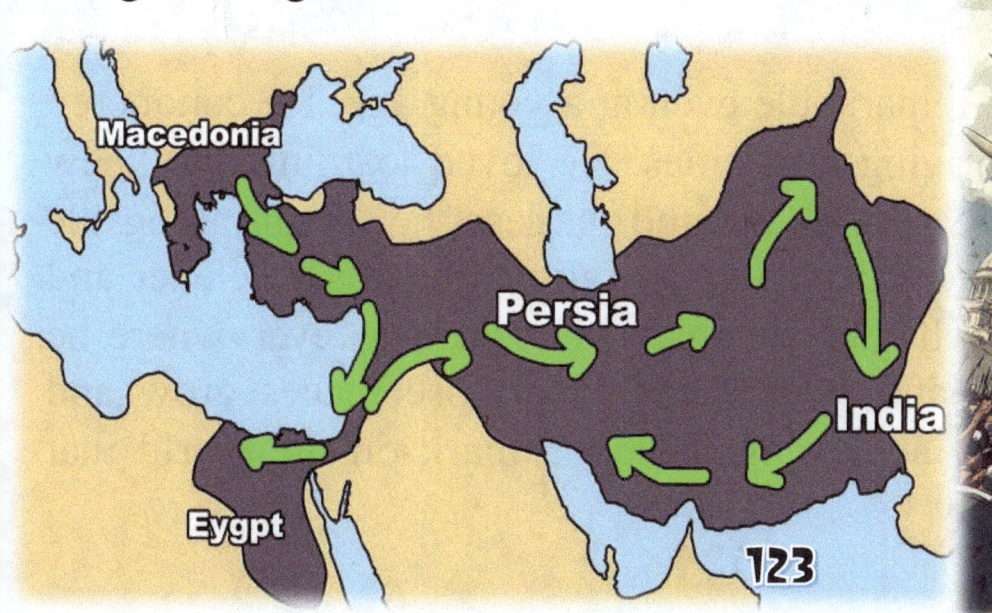

In 323 BC, Alexander was in the city of Babylon (modern-day Iraq). He suddenly fell very ill. Some say he caught a terrible fever, while others believe he may have been poisoned. For several days, Alexander couldn't eat or drink much, and his body grew weaker. Even his brave heart couldn't fight off the illness. Sadly, after almost two weeks of suffering, Alexander passed away.

After his death, his army generals began fighting over the empire and who would take charge. Without Alexander, his vast empire splintered into pieces.

Alexander the Great was remarkable even at a young age. He conquered vast empires and built thriving new cities. He loved learning and knew how important knowledge was. Brave and fearless, he fought alongside his soldiers, earning their loyalty and admiration. He was so clever and smart that he never lost a battle! He shared Greek ideas everywhere he went, like art, language, and science, helping those places grow and learn. His adventures and achievements left a mark on the world that people still talk about today

# The Life of Squirrels

Have you ever seen a squirrel before? They're such cute little animals, aren't they? Squirrels are playful, smart, and hardworking creatures. You'll find them almost anywhere there are trees—like in parks, forests, or even in your backyard! They love living in trees because trees give them food, a cozy shelter, and plenty of space to jump, play, and explore.

A mother squirrel takes great care of her babies. She keeps them safe, warm, and well-fed while they're little. As they grow, she teaches them all the important squirrel skills, like how to find food, collect it, and hide it for later. Once the babies are ready, the mother lets them go off and explore the world.

Squirrels love to eat nuts like acorns and walnuts, but they also enjoy fruits like apples or berries; they can munch on mushrooms lying around in the forest. They're all about healthy meals to stay strong and active!

Squirrels often hide food like nuts and seeds by burying them in the ground. However, they know that other animals, such as birds or other squirrels, are watching and might steal their food. To outsmart these thieves, squirrels sometimes dig empty holes and pretend to hide food. These "trick holes" confuse any sneaky watchers.

A squirrel's teeth keep growing all the time! To stop them from getting too big, squirrels need to chew and gnaw on things. If they didn't, their teeth could grow so long that they wouldn't be able to close their mouths or eat!

Some squirrels can glide through the air as if they're flying! They're known as flying squirrels. But wait, they don't have wings! Instead, they have special skin flaps between their arms and legs that function like a parachute, helping them glide from tree to tree.

Believe it or not, humans were inspired by flying squirrels to create the **WingSuit**, which people use to glide through the air during **BASE jumps**. So, in a way, flying squirrels helped teach people how to "fly"!

# HOW COMPUTERS THINK?

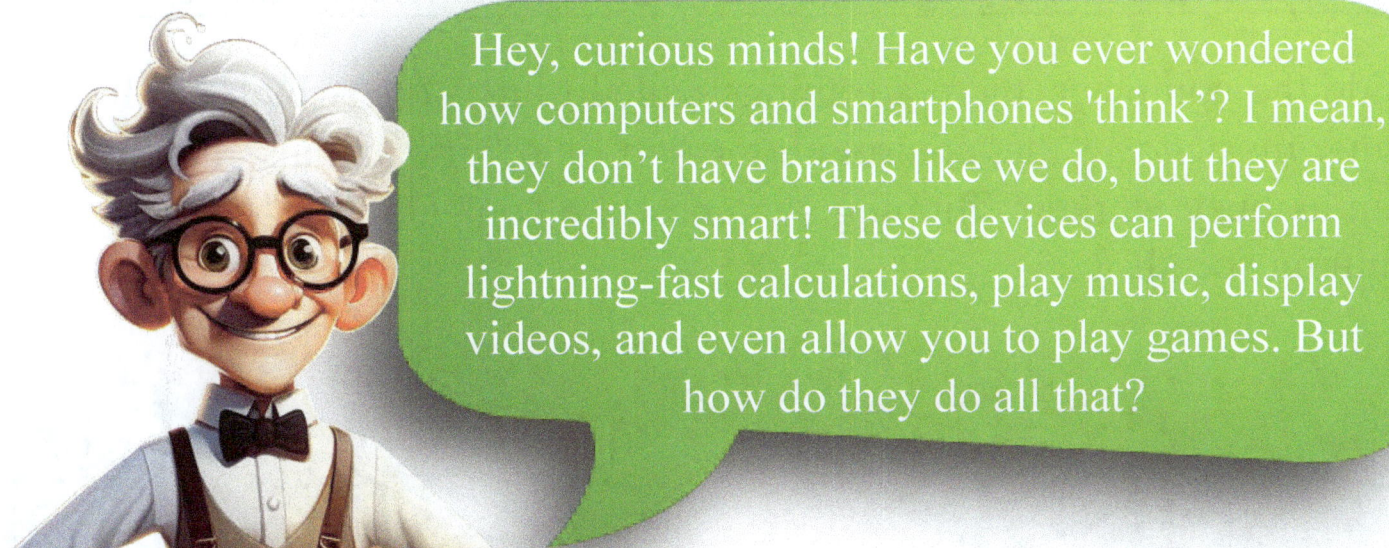

Hey, curious minds! Have you ever wondered how computers and smartphones 'think'? I mean, they don't have brains like we do, but they are incredibly smart! These devices can perform lightning-fast calculations, play music, display videos, and even allow you to play games. But how do they do all that?

## Binary system

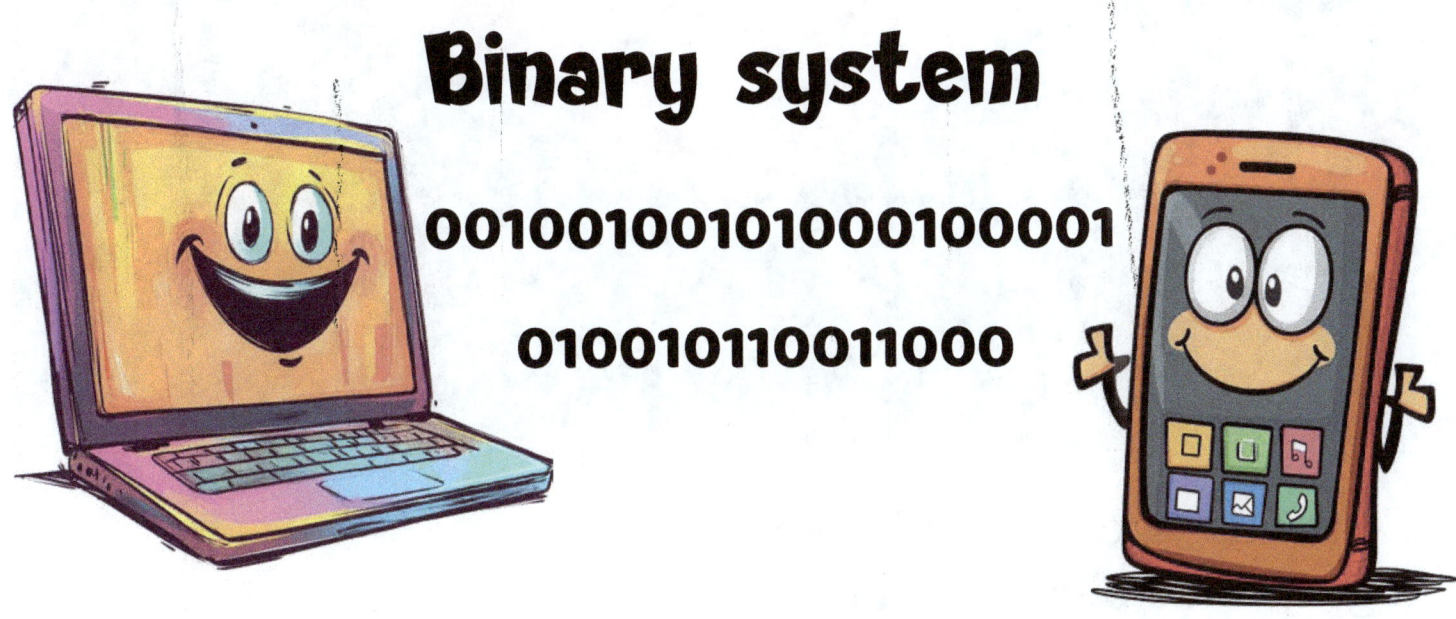

0010010010100010001

010010110011000

Here's the cool part: instead of reading letters, words, or pictures as we do, they understand everything in a super simple way—using only two numbers: **1** and **0**. That's right, just these two! This magical system of 1s and 0s is called **The Binary System**, and it's how computers talk, think, and do all their amazing tricks.

In the world of computers, the numbers **1** and **0** represent two states:
- **1** means something is **on** (like a light switch being turned on).
- **0** means something is **off** (like a light switch being turned off).

Inside the computer, there are things called transistors, which are like *teeny-tiny switches* that control all the "on" and "off" signals. Think of them as busy workers, flipping switches like "on" (1) and "off" (0) at lightning speed!

Computers group these 1s and 0s together into **bits** and **bytes**.
- **1 bit** is just a single **1** or **0**.
- **8 bits** make up **1 byte**, and computers use these bytes to represent letters, numbers, or symbols.

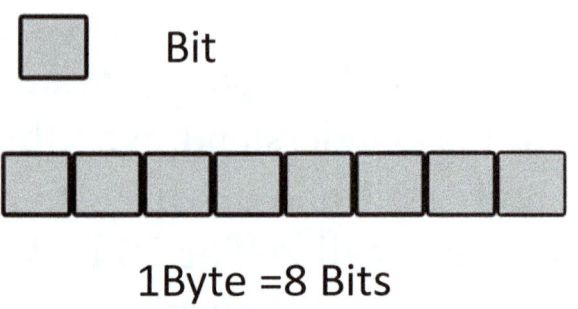

Let's start with an example: a byte has 8 spots, so we could have something like **00000001**. That's a 1 in binary! Or how about **00000010**? That's a 2! The more you mix those 1s and 0s, the bigger the number. It's like stacking blocks; each one makes the number grow higher!

| | | |
|---|---|---|
| 128 64 32 16 8 4 2 **1** <br> 0 0 0 0 0 0 0 1 | **00000001** | Equals number 1 |
| 128 64 32 16 8 4 **2** 1 <br> 0 0 0 0 0 0 1 0 | **00000010** | Equals number 2 |
| 128 64 32 16 8 4 **2 1** <br> 0 0 0 0 0 0 1 1 | **00000011** | Equals number 3 |
| 128 64 32 16 8 **4** 2 1 <br> 0 0 0 0 0 1 0 0 | **00000100** | Equals number 4 |
| 128 64 32 16 8 **4** 2 **1** <br> 0 0 0 0 0 1 0 1 | **00000101** | Equals number 5 |
| 128 64 32 16 8 **4 2** 1 <br> 0 0 0 0 0 1 1 0 | **00000110** | Equals number 6 |
| 128 64 32 16 8 **4 2 1** <br> 0 0 0 0 0 1 1 1 | **00000111** | Equals number 7 |

**Can you guess what these binary numbers equal to?**

# Rainbows

Have you ever seen a rainbow in the sky after a rainy day or near a waterfall? Have you ever wondered how those beautiful rainbows appear in the sky? To understand a rainbow, you first need to know what a **Prism** is!

A **Prism** is a solid piece of glass or plastic shaped like a triangle. It bends light when light passes through it, splitting it into different colors.

Do you remember Isaac Newton, the brilliant scientist who discovered gravity? Well, he also helped us understand how rainbows are formed!

Newton discovered that when white light (like sunlight) passes through a piece of glass with angled surfaces, called a prism, the light splits into a spectrum of colors, the same colors you see in a rainbow.

This occurs because the prism bends light through a process known as refraction, with each color bends by a slightly different degree. The result is a stunning array of colors: red, orange, yellow, green, blue, indigo, and violet.

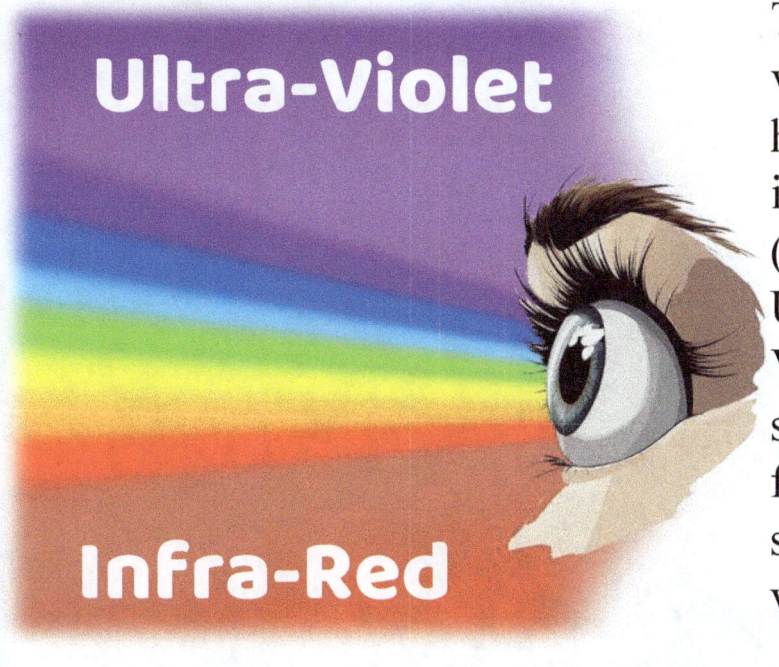

The colors of the rainbow are called visible light, but there are colors the human eye can't see. Beyond violet is Ultraviolet (UV), and infrared (IR) below the red color.

UV light helps the body make Vitamin D, but too much can cause skin burns. Infrared is the heat we feel near a fire. Special cameras can see infrared light, giving them night-vision 'superpowers'

To create the rainbow we see in the sky, something in the air needs to work like a prism—and that something is water droplets! These droplets float in the air after a rainy day near a waterfall, a fountain, or even a backyard sprinkler. Sunlight may look white, but it's actually made up of the many different colors of rainbow!

The raindrop bends sunlight (this phenomenon is known as refraction). Inside the raindrop, the light bounces around (this process is referred to as reflection). When the light exits the raindrop, it splits into all its hidden colors, the colors of the rainbow (this process is called dispersion).

And voilà, a rainbow is born with its amazing and beautiful colors!

# Heart Electricity

Electricity isn't just something that powers our gadgets and gizmos; it's also present in nature and in our own bodies! Yes, my little learners, the human body generates its own electricity, and it absolutely needs it to keep everything running smoothly.

Now, let's talk about one of the most important parts of our body: the heart! Think of it as a super-powerful pump that keeps blood zooming around your body. But here's the truly shocking part (pun intended): the human heart works on electricity! That's right, your heart has its own electrical system to keep it beating in perfect rhythm. !

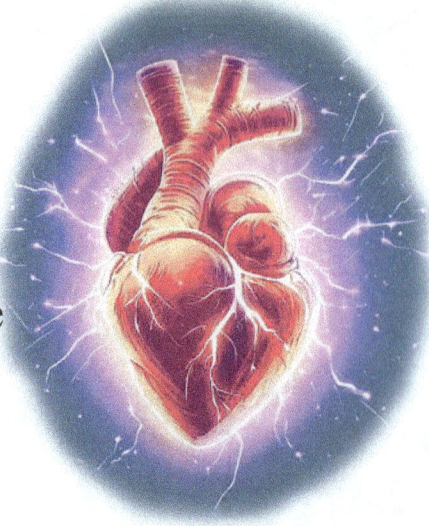

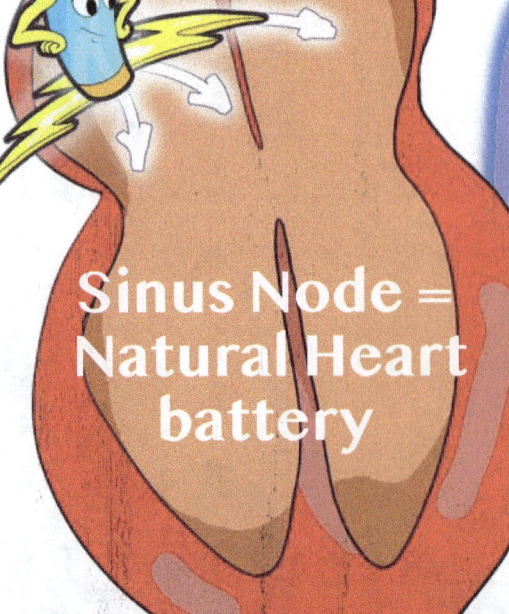

Sinus Node = Natural Heart battery

The heart has four small chambers, and in one of the top chambers is the heart's natural battery, called the **Sinus Node**. This sinus node sends tiny electric signals that travel through the heart muscle, making it beat. The sinus node can work very fast when we're excited, scared, or exercising, and it slows down when we're sleeping or resting

The heart is truly an electrifying organ! Its electrical signals can be recorded using special machines called EKGs or ECGs, where doctors place tiny wires known as electrodes on your chest to pick up the heart's electrical activity.

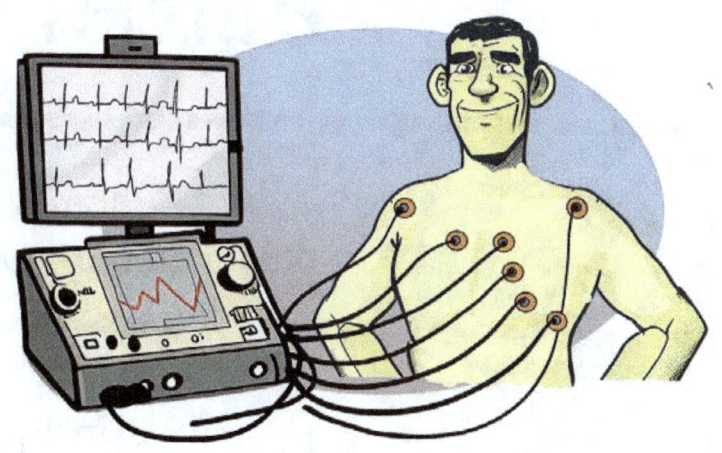

Then, voila! The machine records your heart's rhythm in a way that helps doctors check how well it's doing. Each spike on the EKG represents a heartbeat! That's right every time your heart goes *thump-thump*, it creates a little electrical signal, and the EKG records it as a spike.

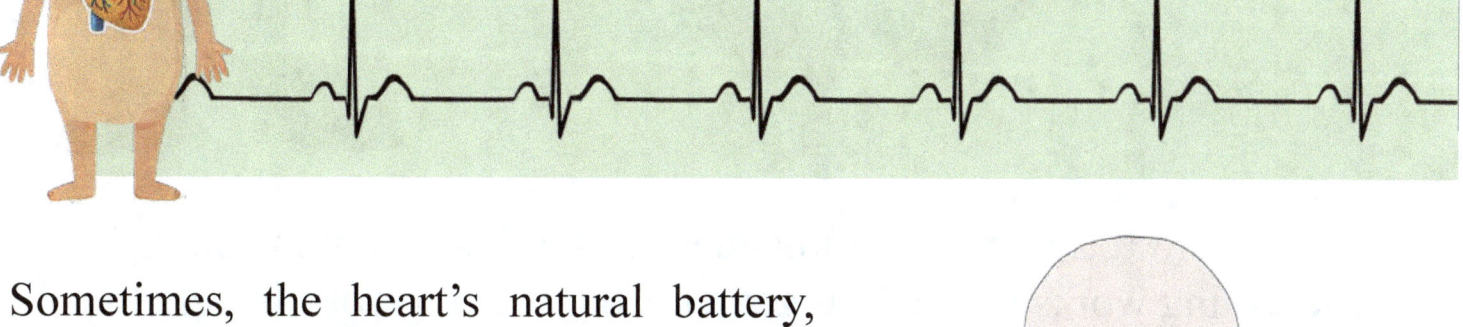

Sometimes, the heart's natural battery, the Sinus Node that keeps it beating, can slow down. But don't worry! Doctors have a clever solution: artificial heart batteries called **Pacemakers**. These tiny devices are implanted under the skin and connected to the heart with special wires. They work like a backup system, keeping the heart beating normally and ensuring everything runs smoothly. Isn't modern medicine amazing?

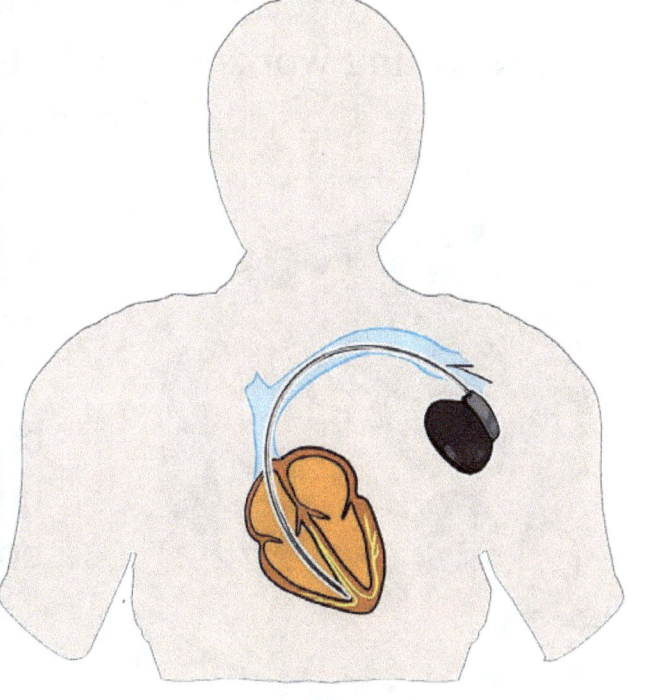

# Human Brain

Imagine having the most powerful computer in the world. And guess what? You already do! It's called your **Brain**, and it lives inside you head.

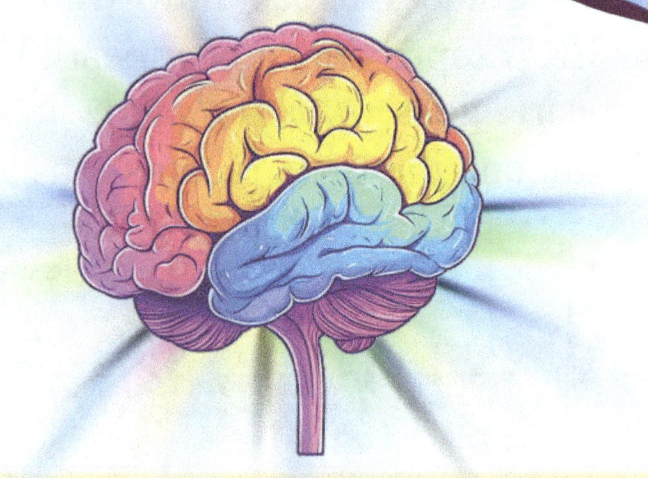

Your brain is like the commander of your body, making sure everything works perfectly together, from moving your fingers to thinking big thoughts.

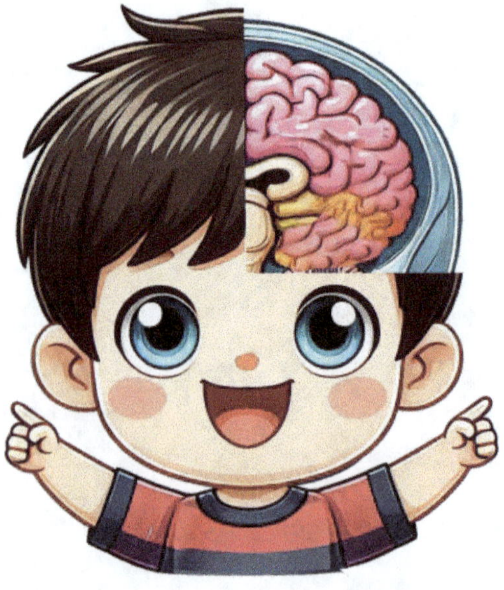

Your brain is so important that it has its own superhero helmet—your **skull**! This super-strong bone protects your brain from getting hurt if you fall or bump your head. It's like your brain's bodyguard, always keeping it safe.

## How the Brain Makes Decisions

Your brain is a decision-making genius! It gathers information from the world around you using your **eyes**, **ears**, **hands**, and other body parts. Then, it processes all that information to decide what to do next. Let's break it down with a fun example:

You're **Hungry**! Your stomach sends a signal to your brain saying, "Hey, I'm hungry! What should I eat?" Your eyes get to work: Your eyes look around the room and spot some delicious food in the kitchen. The brain makes a plan: Your brain thinks, "Let's go to the kitchen and grab that food!"

**Muscles Spring Into Action:** Your brain sends a command to your leg muscles to walk to the kitchen and to your arm and hand to grab the food. **Yum Time!** Your brain even helps to chew and digest the food once it's in your mouth. Talk about a multitasker!

How does the brain function like that? Believe it or not, just like a real computer, the brain operates using **Electricity!**

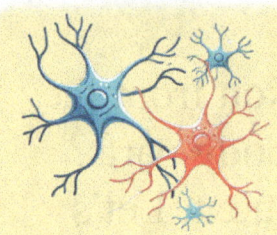

The brain contains millions or even billions of what we call brain cells or **Neurons.**

These neurons look like tiny octopuses with many arms connecting. These brain cells are the key to how the brain functions. They communicate with one another through electrical signals and chemical messengers.

These neurons love to chat with each other, and they do this using their magical 'octopus hands." Where these hands meet to share their secrets is called a synapse. Think of a synapse as a little bridge between neurons. When you learn something new, like how to whistle or ride a bike, your brain builds more of these bridges so neurons can send messages faster and better. And guess what? The more you use your brain to solve puzzles, read books (just like this one!), or try new things, the more bridges your neurons will build. Cool, right?

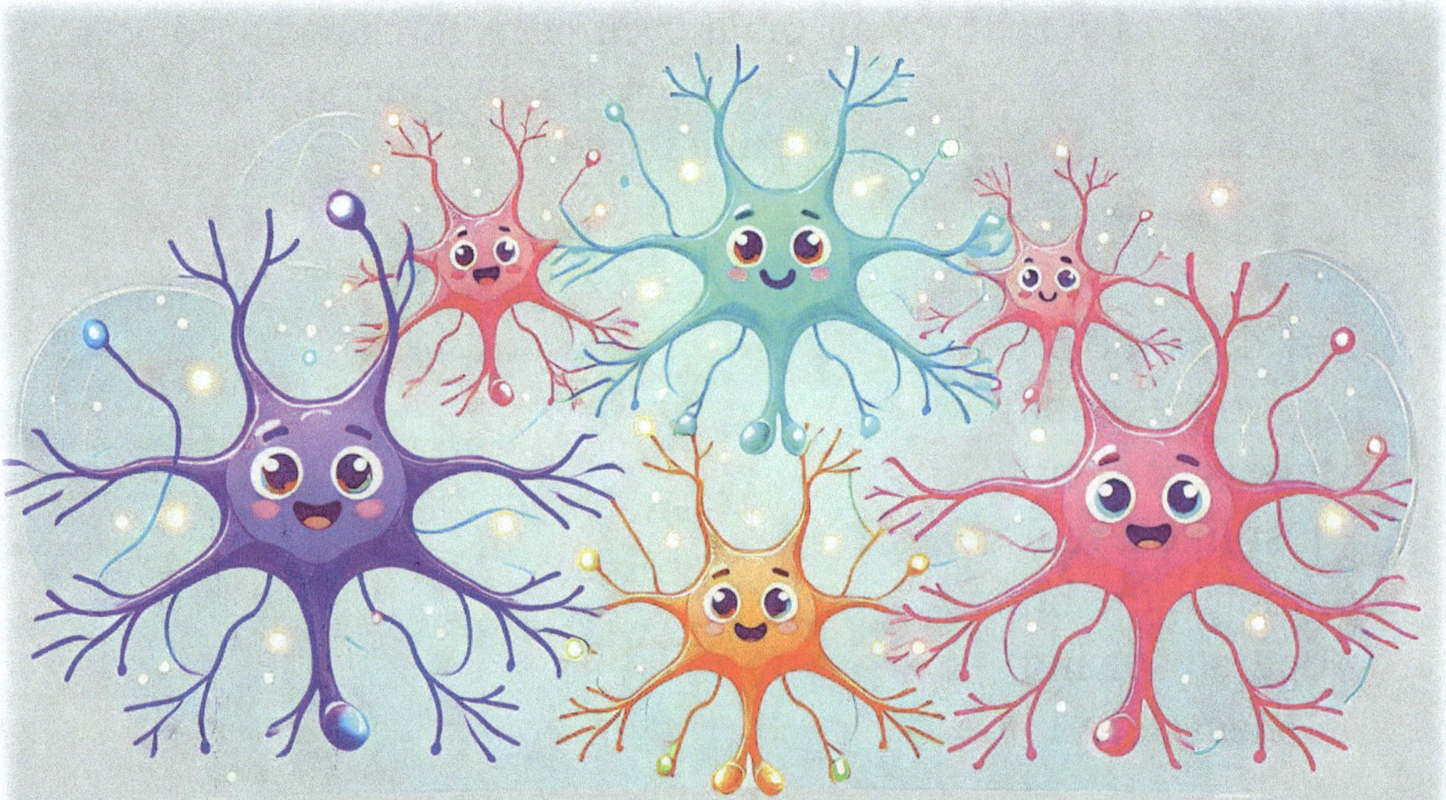

# Healthy habits

Caring for your heart, brain, and entire body is extremely important! Here are some tips on how you can keep them strong and healthy for a long time:

**Eat Healthy Food**: Fill your plate with fruits, veggies, and other yummy, nutritious foods. It's like fuel for your superhero body!

**Get Moving:** Exercise daily—run, jump, dance, or play your favorite sport. Your heart loves it when you stay active!

**Sleep Well:** Ensure you have a restful night's sleep. Your body and mind require rest to recharge and become stronger.

**Drink Water.** Your heart loves water! Staying hydrated helps your blood flow easily, so drink plenty of water throughout the day, especially when you're running around.

**Don't Smoke or Vape** Smoking and vaping can hurt your heart and lungs. So, say "no thanks" if anyone offers you these things.

When you do all these things, your heart and brain will thank you by staying healthy and happy for years to come!

# Nobel Prize

On a sunny morning in 1888, **Alfred Nobel** was drinking his morning coffee and reading a French newspaper when he received shocking news. The newspaper mistakenly reported that he had died! "I am definitely not dead," he told himself. But what upset him the most was how the article "The Merchant of Death " described him. This phrase deeply saddened Alfred, as it suggested that his life's work had caused harm rather than good.

Let us trace back to learn more about this remarkable man, Alfred Nobel, and discover why his name became so famous!

Long ago, people needed explosive materials to dig holes in mountains and rocks while building railways and cities. They used black powder, an easy-to-make explosive, but it wasn't strong or safe.

140

Later, they discovered a liquid substance called **nitroglycerin**, a highly potent explosive. However, nitroglycerin was extremely dangerous; just a slight shake could cause it to explode! In the 1860s, Alfred Nobel, a Swedish chemist, decided to tackle this problem.

He wanted to find a way to make nitroglycerin safer to handle. After years of experimentation, he found that when nitroglycerin was mixed with a specific powder, it became less volatile and much safer to handle. This mixture could be shaped into sticks for easy use.

He named his invention **dynamite**, naming it after the Greek word **dynamis**, which means "power."

Nobel's invention of dynamite became a game-changer. It was much safer than liquid nitroglycerin, easy to transport, and incredibly powerful. Dynamite was used for building railways, tunnels, and roads, as well as for mining and clearing out old buildings or rock formations. It quickly became a global success, making Alfred Nobel a very wealthy man.

Unfortunately, while Nobel intended dynamite for peaceful purposes such as construction and mining, it was quickly adopted for military use. Soldiers utilized it in battles to destroy their enemies. This deeply upset Nobel, as he never intended his invention to cause harm. Furthermore, when a French newspaper mistakenly published his death news.

He started to think that he did not want to be remembered as the person who invented war weapons that led to more destruction and casualties. Nobel devoted his money and fortune to something positive; he did not want to be remembered as the merchant of death. So, he set aside most of his wealth to create the **Nobel Prizes!**

The **Nobel Prize** is considered one of the most prestigious awards worldwide and throughout human history. It is given to individuals who are carefully selected for their outstanding contributions to humanity and efforts to make the world a better place. The recipients of this incredible honor are called Nobel Prize Laureates. Every year, Nobel Prizes are awarded in the fields of Peace, Physics, Chemistry, Medicine, Literature, and Economic Sciences. Winners are invited to attend a grand ceremony mainly in **Stockholm, Sweden**, where they are celebrated for their achievements in front of a distinguished scientific and global community.

Imagine one day you work so hard in your field that you get to stand in front of a cheering crowd, accepting your very own Nobel Prize! The winners receive not only a significant monetary reward but also a beautiful gold medal engraved with the image of Alfred Nobel himself.

As humanity, we have discovered and learned so much about our history and our planet, but there is still so much more that we do not know. There are stories from the past, and even from recent history, that we can't be sure about. Are they just myths, or are they real events?

Today, we're going to talk about one of those mysterious stories: the tale of the Lost City of **Atlantis.**

# Between Myth and Reality

# Atlantis

2,500 years ago in ancient Greece, a great philosopher named **Plato** lived. He was renowned for his wisdom and knowledge, but he began speaking about something extraordinary one day. He described a magnificent city that existed on an island in the ocean about 9,000 years before his time. This city was the legendary Atlantis. According to Plato, Atlantis was a breathtaking place filled with wonders beyond what people could imagine, a utopia of wealth, technology, and culture like no other.

Atlantis was said to have been built on a magnificent island. It was a city like no other, with a splendor that captured the imagination of many. It was a powerful and wealthy kingdom surrounded by the endless blue of the ocean. The city was adorned with majestic temples, grand palaces, and lush gardens that sparkled like jewels under the sun.

Legends describe Atlantis as far ahead of its time. Its architecture, art, and technology were unmatched by any other civilization. Some tales even speak of flying machines and advanced sciences, all of which existed 9,000 years before the time of the great philosopher Plato.

The people of Atlantis were believed to be incredibly wise, living in harmony with nature and each other. They cherished peace, valued knowledge, and made science and learning the cornerstone of their prosperous society. Atlantis wasn't just a city but a beacon of what humanity could achieve at its best.

Over time, the Atlanteans became greedy and corrupt, losing their virtuous ways as they obsessed over power and material wealth. They sought domination over other lands and transformed into a society characterized by arrogance and conquest. Then one day, the sky darkened, an enormous earthquake shook the city, and gigantic waves swallowed it whole. Atlantis was lost beneath the sea in the blink of an eye!

he legend of Atlantis is often seen as a metaphor, teaching us that even the most powerful civilizations can fall if they lose their values, become greedy, or succumb to corruption. It remains a mystery to this day whether Atlantis truly existed or was a story created by the philosopher Plato to illustrate an important moral lesson. Some believe Atlantis might have been located in the vast Atlantic Ocean, while others think it could have been in the Mediterranean Sea. Many explorers and researchers have searched for clues to its existence, fueled by the possibility that a real place may have inspired the story. However, others argue that Atlantis is simply a myth, a tale woven to warn humanity about the consequences of losing integrity and balance.

**The End.**

Alright, kids! We've reached the end of this part of our journey. But don't worry; more adventures are just around the corner! Stay tuned for a brand new Encyclopedia One Adventure coming your way soon in the next volume.

Great care has been taken to ensure this book contains verified and accurate information. If you believe any part of this book contains inaccuracies, don't hesitate to get in touch with the author.